If all that this book accomplished was to paint a vision for how self-directed learning could become accessible to all kids who find school soul-crushing, that alone would be a huge contribution to our desperate public discourse on education. Learning via the pursuit of one's joys is a privilege available to few—mostly to those whose parents unearth both the courage and the resourcefulness needed. The miracles of unschooling have typically been individual miracles concerning individual families and individual kids. So, even just nudging our collective consciousness to imagine how we could do better—that in itself would be quite something.

The amazing thing is, Ken and his friend Josh did their own imagining for a few months in 1996, then they promptly got on with the practicalities. They quit their middle school teaching jobs and opened a radically new kind of center.

For over 20 years, North Star: Self-Directed Learning for Teens has been making joyful, inspired, consent-based learning possible for every youth in the vicinity who wants to try it (and, of course, whose parents are willing to give it a chance). Ken and his team have accrued an astounding body of stories and wisdom, from nitty-gritty to existential to unexpected and uplifting. In person, Ken is a delightful human—funny, sincere, blunt, generous, and understated. I'm thrilled to find that reading his book is just like listening to him talk.

– Grace Llewellyn
Executive Director, The Hive: Self-Directed Learning for Teens
Founder and Director, Not Back to School Camp
Author of *The Teenage Liberation Handbook*

North Star is a revolutionary alternative for teenagers who don't click with traditional school: not quite homeschooling, not quite an alternative school, and financially accessible to all. Ken's story of founding (and spreading) the North Star model offers hope and inspiration for anxious parents, disgruntled educators, and curious students who know there must be a better way."

– Blake Boles
Founder of *Unschool Adventures*
Author of *The Art of Self-Directed Learning;*
Better Than College; and *College Without High School.*

Learning is Natural, School is Optional.

The North Star approach to offering teens a head start on life

By Kenneth Danford

Published by Golden Door Press

Sunderland, Massachusetts

Learning is Natural, School Is Optional:
The North Star approach to offering teens a head start on life
ISBN-13: 978-1-7335490-0-4

PRINTED IN THE U.S.A.

Published by Golden Door Press
P.O. Box 21
Sunderland, MA 01375
Email: author@kennethdanford.com

Learn more about North Star: Self-Directed Learning for Teens at http://www.northstarteens.org, and about Liberated Learners at http://wwww.liberatedlearners.net.

DISCLAIMER: Although every effort was made to ensure that the content of this book is accurate and up to date, no part of it should be construed as legal advice. All contents are the opinion and based on the experience of the author, who is not an attorney or legal advisor. All risk associated with following the guidance in this book is borne solely by the reader. Always check applicable laws applying to any location before you seek to start an alternative learning program, and observe all laws and restrictions.

Image credits:
Front Cover Photo by Loran Saito
Photos by Jodi Lyn Cutler: Pages 16, 140, 218 top, 242
Photos by Kim Chin-Gibbons: Pages 166, 208, 218 bottom
Author Photo by Richie Davis: Page 248
Photo of Author and Joshua Hornick, page 50: unknown

This book is dedicated to:

- *All the North Star alumni and current members who chose to leave the known path of school for the uncertainties of self-directed learning, trusting North Star to be their guide and support system.*

- *All staff and volunteers who have made North Star a vibrant, beautiful, and inspirational community over these years.*

- *All the friends and donors who have contributed to North Star because they feel some resonance and inspiration with our mission and want us to grow.*

- *All those who pioneered homeschooling, unschooling, and self-directed learning in the 1970s, 1980s, and 1990s, to show that—yes, indeed—there is another way to grow up and thrive.*

- *And, for all teens and their parents reading this book, who currently feel trapped in school and don't know how to make it through one more day or one more year, and for whom high school graduation is too far away. Mostly, this book is for you.*

CONTENTS

Under the flickering light of the North Star,
behind some craggy hill or snow-covered mountain,
stood a doubtful freedom — half-frozen —
beckoning us to come and share its hospitality.

– Engraved in Frederick Douglass Circle monument
at the northwest corner of Central Park,
New York City

1

Who Knew?

Who knew that the best answer to all of the stressful demands on the current American teen—getting good grades, finding a serious passion, building a strong resumé for college applications, wondering what to study in college, fearing how to pay for college, or considering an alternative to college—is a simple, powerful, and profound action: Stop going to school.

It's one thing to know this surprising truth, and to declare that school is optional. It's another thing entirely to make school optional for any interested teen.

What does it take to offer a viable and inspiring alternative to attending school? How do teens go from feeling trapped to feeling in control of their lives? How do teens thrive without traditional high school diplomas?

The answers are not secrets, and they are not complicated. In fact, many of us live this way every day. It's just a matter of making it possible for any interested teen to join us.

That's the story we have to tell at North Star: Self-Directed Learning for Teens.

Our Name

We have had good luck with names. When we first created our program, we took the name Pathfinder Learning Center, based on the local private family non-profit organization—The Pathfinder Foundation—that adopted us.

After six years of positive interaction, we decided to incorporate our own non-profit organization, and had to come up with a new name.

Our Board of Directors and staff had many discussions, searching for the right replacement. I remember feeling content with Pathfinder, and discouraged at losing both such an apt title, as well as the name recognition we had developed to that point.

At one brainstorming session, then-Board Member John Sprague shared his friend's suggestion of "North Star." That sounded bold to me. My immediate U.S. history teacher reaction was, "The Underground Railroad! Frederick Douglass' newspaper! Liberation!" and then, "We can't compare school to slavery." I was both thrilled and fearful that we were overreaching.

Interestingly enough, the non-history teachers in the room had an entirely different first response. "Navigation and orienteering! Helping people who are lost! Stability and reliability in the universe!" They heard the "Pathfinder" sentiment of the North Star as a compass or guide, a wonderful continuity as we changed names.

These responses continue to thrill me. Frederick Douglass is one of my heroes of U.S. history. His 1852 speech about July Fourth is part of my annual celebration of that holiday. The characters of the Underground Railroad fill me with courage and inspiration. After reading *Bound for Canaan* by Fergus Bordewich, my newest personal hero is Levi Coffin, informally known as the "President of the Underground Railroad." Helping teens take control of their lives makes me connect with this part of U.S. history.

At the same time, I am filled with joy at being the stable, reliable constant that offers calm and orientation to those in crisis. In the context of astronomy, the North Star is the first essential item to identify. For many local families, finding North Star has been an important moment in discovering some direction and reassurance.

From Pathfinder to North Star, these names have given us a lot to live up to in our work. They are lofty visions for a program. Names may not make the program, but in this case, they have been a very good place to start.

2

What Do I Do For A Living?

I originally wrote this section in 2002, to introduce a booklet of essays written by North Star members about their experiences. I have edited and updated it for this book. – K.D.

Frequently, an unsuspecting new friend or acquaintance innocently asks me, "What do you do for a living?"

I usually pause to buy time, size up how much they might really want to hear, and then launch into some explanation of North Star. In more than twenty years, I doubt I have ever used the same description twice, and rarely have I been concise. In fact, after all of these years, many of my own extended family members and close friends still don't fully understand what I do.

One plausible answer that I can use to avoid complications is that I run an alternative school for teenagers. However, North Star is not a school by any means. Legally it is not a school, organizationally it is not a school, and spiritually it is not a school. Further, the phrase "alternative school" screams out connotations of a place for people who could not make it in regular school. Until we change that cultural norm, I cringe at the term and the assumptions it elicits.

A second response that is easy for people to understand is that I run a community center for homeschooling teenagers. While this is closer to the mark in many ways, North Star has been a program for existing homeschoolers only in a fortuitous sort of way.

North Star uses the legal mechanism of homeschooling to provide teenagers the space and time to discover their own interests and passions. It is true that all members of North Star under sixteen are legally homeschoolers, but that is directly because we helped the vast majority of them leave school to undertake this approach.

North Star has always been blessed to have among its members a group of lifelong homeschoolers who came to this lifestyle independently of us, but these families were not the people whose lives Joshua Hornick and I were aiming to change when we left public school teaching. While we have many connections with the local homeschooling community, we are not fully integrated with that group, and many local homeschoolers thrive without becoming members of North Star.

Meanwhile, when I use the word "homeschooling" to describe what I do, I often see my listeners become disinterested, skeptical, or concerned that we are a threat to quality public schools. To say the least, using the term "homeschooling" has not provided clarity to the genuinely interested inquirer.

There is a wing of the homeschooling movement that believes teenagers will grow into thoughtful and mature adults with enough trust, opportunities, and gentle guidance, without replicating the curriculum of school at home. The term for this approach is "unschooling," and to me it means choosing what to learn based on one's interests, rather than on what students the same age are learning in schools. Thus, a third answer to what I do for a living is that I run a center that promotes unschooling for teenagers.

While I personally find this a satisfying response, most people I try this one on don't have the slightest clue what I mean. Then I find myself backpedaling, covering for the unpleasant reality that 'unschooling' sounds somewhat negative and snide to many people unfamiliar with the phrase. I now use this answer cautiously.

The fourth possibility is the shock option. Sometimes, for fun, I will say that for a living, I encourage teenagers to quit school. People don't know whether I'm joking or serious. I used this with great amusement once at my friend's wedding reception, where a young woman my friend and I were seated with insisted on telling us that for her job she worked as a stripper. She was more annoying than convincing, so I decided to say, "Well, you may be a stripper, but I coach junior high age kids to drop out of school."

She was horrified, and snatched the photos of her children away so I couldn't see them, confessing, "All right, I'll tell you the truth: I'm not really a stripper."

I smiled and replied, "Well, I really do coach kids to drop out of school."

She blurted out, "Has anyone ever tried to assassinate you?"

Needless to say, I rarely employ this strategy, but in the right setting, I can get a big kick out of it.

The fifth response I sometimes use to explain my work is to roll out a mission statement-type response. I declare, "I make living and learning without school a viable and inspiring option for any interested teen in the Pioneer Valley," or perhaps, "I encourage teenagers to become mature and competent young adults through an educational approach called self-directed learning."

The silence that often follows can be uncomfortable. Either the questioner doesn't understand this gibberish, or they think I am a New Age healer. In any case, this formal response is usually unappealing.

In the luxury of this space, I will say that what I do for a living is change lives. I introduce people to a different lifestyle that offers challenge, inspiration, and reward.

I do my work one family at a time. Mostly, I work with teenagers, but I work with parents, as well. How I work with each teen is directly dependent on who their parents are, and what they deem important for their teen. I work with family units, and I am successful only when both teens and parents feel satisfied with the changes in their lives.

North Star as a center offers the services that are essential to families for them to embark on this shift in lifestyle. The infrastructure of North Star is the minimum needed to permit teens and parents to feel comfortable with the idea of leaving school. The average member stays about two years, by which time they have the confidence and direction necessary to pursue their lives, often at ages much younger than the common high school graduation age of eighteen years old.

My work is helping people to believe in themselves, and to believe there is a space for them in our society. My job is to open things up for them right now, and convince them that they do not need to wait until they are eighteen and hold a high school diploma to begin their lives. I know that school is optional, and I understand that many people have found success in many ways, independent of their school experiences or credentials. I am teaching families that this lifestyle is not just for the odd, the lucky, or the unusually gifted.

At the same time, I am much more than a coach encouraging people to trust themselves. The infrastructure of North Star may be the minimum necessary mentioned above, but it is an impressive infrastructure.

I do teach classes, and the rest of the staff does so, as well. I do find members internships, jobs, and volunteer possibilities. I love tutoring odd topics with members of North Star. I relish the opportunity to create an inviting and safe social space. I embrace the need to expand my knowledge of bookkeeping and accounting. I enjoy answering the phone to see who is calling us today.

The fact that some lifelong unschoolers join North Star every year attests to the strengths of our infrastructure. These people don't need a single pep talk from me, they just want quality services they aren't finding elsewhere. When they choose to join North Star, I take their decision as confirmation of the value of our program.

In 2013, I began my TEDx Talk at Amherst College with the question, "What do you say to a teen who tells you, 'I wish I didn't have to go to school. Isn't there some other way?'"

For me, this question has a painful urgency. In 1996, I needed to create a meaningful answer to that question for myself. I sought a reply that would reflect my assessment of schooling and be immediately usable by the young person asking me this deeply serious question: "Isn't there some other way?"

My own skills, interests, and sense of responsibility guided the development of my answer. This book is the detailed explanation of that process. It is the story of working with others, building a team, creating a community, and improving a program. It is the story of welcoming all interested families with no waiting lists, lotteries, or selective admissions process. It is the story of making yesterday the last day of school for any interested teen.

So, what do I do for a living?

I tell teens and parents, "Yes, there is another way, and we will help you use it. You can start right now."

3

Two Criticisms of Schooling

When I set out to write a book, I did not want to add to the "What's wrong with schools and how to fix them" genre. This genre dates back over a century, to John Dewey, Paul Goodman, Ivan Illich, John Holt, Jonathan Kozol, and a bookstore-worth more, in the past couple of decades.

I do share my own process of disillusionment, from being a successful student to an idealistic teacher to an intended reformer to a conscientious objector, helping others to leave school with me.

Mostly, though, I am choosing to tell the tale of what followed that moment. In this chapter, I offer two relatively mild criticisms of schooling that provide some insight into my thinking. Beyond this point, I intend to offer an original story about how to provide an alternative to our current model.

1. Connect the dots

On the day I was born in 1965, you could have placed a bet that eighteen years from that coming June, I would be graduating from my local public high school. You would have been right. You would also have been right had you made this wager about each of my two brothers, and for that matter, my three cousins. In fact, you could have made this bet a generation earlier, about each of my parents, and a generation later, about each of my children. You could also have made this gamble and been correct about my wife and her brother, along with her parents, and her niece and nephew.

This realization is not as much a criticism of schooling as it is a critique of our culture. We have a fairly narrow script for the first eighteen years of life. I didn't realize how confining our cultural assumptions are, until I resigned from school and started to encourage young people to leave, as well.

Suddenly, we were in unscripted territory. Everything was on the table for North Star members at younger-than-expected ages, and their life paths became somewhat unpredictable.

I was getting people off track in a way that I had never dared to be in my own life before. I was now seeing the familiar, desired, and respectable path of my childhood and my family experience as a version of connect-the-dots or color-by-number: staying within the lines.

For me, this observation of how predictable schooling makes our childhood affects how I feel about the system. The process I enjoyed as I child now seems almost unbearable. I honestly don't know if I could go back and do twelve years of school again.

2. Four Food Groups

A common debate among school reformers is how much schools have changed over the past one hundred years. Some feel that the assumptions, expectations, and demands upon schooling have shifted it beyond recognition from what our parents and grandparents remember about their experiences. I tend to agree with the view that says schools haven't changed very much at all, and see that as a problem.

First, the structure of schooling has hardly changed at all from what my parents experienced in the 1940s and 1950s, and perhaps even from what my grandparents experienced a generation earlier. The structure of school remains a compulsory system that children attend 180 days per year, for twelve years. Within the school, the letter grading system has not changed at all; what's more, the basic curriculum hasn't evolved, either.

I have an analogy to explain my criticism of the schooling curriculum. I believe the school curriculum is generally stuck on a model akin to a nutritional model of my childhood, which our government promoted from 1956-1992.

The Four Food Groups were Grains, Dairy, Meat, and Fruits-Vegetables. These categories compare numerically to the curriculum groups of English, Math, Science, and Social Studies.

Schooling assumes that all children must take courses in all of these "basic subjects" every year, to be supplemented with "electives" such as the arts, foreign languages, and more. Interdisciplinary courses are seen as innovative and creative approaches to engaging students, much like casseroles or one-dish meals that incorporate different food groups into one presentation.

The USDA modified the Four Food Groups in 1992, into the Food Pyramid. I expect most people of my age bracket and older remember the Four Food Groups with some nostalgia, however outdated they may seem now. In fact, many nutritionists contend that the Four Food Groups are misguided or harmful, and recommend a substantially different vision about food categories as our country confronts an obesity epidemic.

To me, the "Core Curriculum" is similarly outdated. What may have been appropriate for my grandparents in the 1920s can't possibly remain the most effective way to categorize information a century later. We can all think of our own updates, revisions, or "Curriculum Pyramid" that we would like to promote.

For me, that might include skill sets around entrepreneurship, freelancing, and self-employment, as global cultures increasingly embrace the "gig" culture in careers. It would likely involve technology and hands-on skills. Given the modern global world, I would promote foreign language acquisition, much as it happens in Europe. I would also include creativity, the arts, and outdoor time as important elements in a curriculum pyramid. Actually, I don't know if I would go with a pyramid at all, to be honest.

I have abandoned the notion that "one curriculum fits all," and I spend my time with teens and families developing individual approaches to learning. I am not particularly interested in "curriculum reform" any more.

I offer this analogy to share my perspective. The rest of this book will not be a criticism of school, nor a blueprint for education reform.

It is, instead, part memoir and part case study. It is the story of creating a twenty-first century program based on our common sense observations and assessments of what teens need to thrive in the modern world.

4

The First Conversation

Ken: Hello, North Star, this is Ken.

Parent: Hello. I need some help, please. My child is resisting going to school, and I don't know what to do. He's a good kid, and he's bright, and he's done fine in school up to now. But he says he's bored, and that it's all pointless. I sort of agree with him, but he can't just stay home. I made him go today, under major threats. We've driven by your building, but we don't really know what goes on there or how it works. We see the kids playing outside, and they look happy. I told him I would call you today.

K: Thank you. You are in the right place. Yes, the kids here are pretty happy, for sure. What is your son's name, and how old is he?

P: He's fourteen, and his name is Matt. He's been going to eighth grade at the regular public school here. We've looked into some private schools, but they are expensive, and I'm not sure he'd like them any better.

K: I see. Does he have any hobbies, or particular interests?

P: Well, he plays some sports, like baseball and skiing. He's pretty social. At school, he used to like to read, and he was into science experiments for a while, but not anymore. And he plays the drums. Oh, and he likes to make money. He's into his computer, and he's helped his grandparents and some family friends set things up as an occasional job.

K: Wow, Matt sounds like a reasonably healthy fourteen-year-old who is just frustrated with school.

P: Yes, exactly. Outside of school and homework, he is a solid guy.

K: Well, this is fantastic. He may really love to hear what we have to offer. North Star proposes that he just stop going to school and do all the things he really likes to do.

P: What? You can do that? He'd be the happiest kid on Earth to hear that.

K: Actually, yes you can. North Star is a community center that helps you file homeschooling papers to become independent from school, and then hosts a program full of classes, tutoring, and people. Matt can come here as much or as little as he wishes, like a YMCA or a club. All of our teens have an advisor, and we help teens construct a weekly routine and set of activities that starts with their strengths and interests.

P: So, we file homeschooling papers, and North Star is not actually a school?

K: Correct. We have lots of people and lots of learning, but we are not legally a school. We don't give credits or diplomas. We don't require attendance.

P: Do the students go on to college? Is this just for troubled kids or dropouts?

K: Actually, about eighty percent of our teens go on to college or other formal programs. Some just take a year or so out of school, then go back to high school. We've been doing this since 1996, and we have alumni who have gone on to all sorts of colleges and careers. It's

*totally healthy. And most of the teens here have some
story like your son's. They attended school, hit a wall,
and didn't know there was another choice. They would
not have opted out of schooling without North Star.
They would have stayed, muddled through high school
unhappily, and graduated, like many people we know.*

P: *Oh, yes. That was me. But really, they can go to college
without going to high school?*

K: *Absolutely. Many of our members start with community
college at ages 15-18 years old, then move on to four-
year colleges ahead of their high school peers. Imagine
spending those teen years doing some part-time college,
pursuing your interests, having a job or internship, and
generally being happy. The adult world welcomes these
teens when they are mature and self-aware 18-year-olds.
In fact, my famous line is, "There is nothing you can do
with a high school diploma that you can't do without
one." This surprises most people.*

P: *Well, it sure surprises me. Does North Star have admissions? What's the process?*

K: *North Star welcomes everyone. We are a non-profit with
a mission of making living and learning without school
a viable and inspiring option for any interested teen in
the Pioneer Valley of western Massachusetts.*

*We do have a fee; it's 40% or less than tuition for pri-
vate schools. We've never turned anyone away because
they couldn't pay the full fee. Also, we've turned no one
away for being a hard case, or for their prior behavior or
academic records in school. We've welcomed every family that has ever wanted to join.*

*The next step would be for you to come in with Matt,
have a look around, and have a face-to-face meeting*

with me. If you like what you see, then today can be Matthew's last day of school.

P: *You can't see me, but I want you to know I'm weeping. Can we come in tomorrow?*

Since the summer of 1996, when Joshua Hornick and I started Pathfinder Learning Center (which became North Star: Self-Directed Learning for Teens, in 2002), I have had conversations like this one with perhaps two thousand parents. My family, friends, and colleagues know that I do not seem to grow tired of these conversations. For me, each phone call is a fresh opportunity to make a significant difference in the life of a teen and their family.

The goal of this first contact is to inform parents and teens that they are not trapped in school, that there is a solution to their situation that they likely have not considered, and that North Star exists to make this choice possible for them.

Best of all, this choice is available immediately, with no applications, admissions, or financial obstacles. When I am making this offer to a family in distress, I feel that I am doing important work, and I can't think of any task I'd rather be doing.

In this book, I will share how I created this role for myself, and what is needed to make the offer fully meaningful to the families with whom I am speaking.

My Story

I grew up in Shaker Heights, Ohio, and attended public school with joy and success. I took mostly Advanced Placement classes in high school, and graduated with honors and a high class-rank. To be honest, though, I only recall a few teachers being particularly necessary and effective for my learning. I had the same math teacher, Mr. Ray Skitzki, for three consecutive years, and he guided our group through advanced math and calculus.

I remember each unit, I would feel confused by a new theory or technique, and that Mr. Skitzki had a calm and patient mantra as he wandered about his classroom: "Struggle with it." I found that eventually things clicked, and in those moments I appreciated his patience in allowing me the time and space to figure it out on my own. I eventually scored a "5" on the BC Calculus Advanced Placement exam, surely a high point of my high school academic career.

I also had the same Latin teacher for four years, Dr. Henry Strater. The class content was moderately useful, and I enjoyed this long-term relationship with Dr. Strater. He was also the coach for the Debate Team, of which I was a member all those years, and I saw him spend his weekend days traveling with us to tournaments. I could see he valued more about his work than simply the classroom learning he offered.

I had a handful of other good classes, I suppose, but none that altered my interests and life course. I didn't complain too much about school or the workload. I didn't imagine having options, so school was something to manage and master. I was able to do so without much stress, and I generally felt satisfied with my life at that time.

More importantly to me than the classroom learning, my group of friends and our mentors created the Shaker Heights High School Student Group on Race Relations in 1983; an organization that continues its work today, and is now the largest club at the school.

At the time, the student body of Shaker Heights High School was approximately half white, half African-American, with a small but growing number of Asian and Latino students. However, much of daily life for students inside the building was segregated.

The advanced classes were predominantly white. Many of the sports teams and clubs were identified as being for one race or the other. Even the cafeteria had its sections. Worse, outside of school, most students did not have integrated social groups, and those groups that crossed racial lines faced both negative peer pressure and perhaps even concerns from their families.

Due mostly to our mentor, Zachary Green, my after-school peer counseling group was integrated. Many of us also participated on the Debate Team, another integrated group. We faced many of the pressures and discomforts of crossing the racial boundary lines on a social basis. The academically achieving African-American students faced the most stress, but we all had stories to share.

In our junior year, the school offered a one-hour race relations program to help stimulate conversation about this situation, and we were angry that this assembly seemed about the limit of what the school was prepared to do. With Zachary's help, we positioned ourselves to become the follow-up group to pursue race relations.

We decided that this problem was a difficult one to solve with our peers, but could be addressed with younger students. We had experienced that cross-racial friendships were accepted in elementary school, but tended to dissolve under the pressures of junior high school and high school. We figured we could go talk to sixth-graders, and encourage them to act with more awareness and purpose regarding their friendship decisions as they transitioned out of elementary school.

We created The Student Group on Race Relations (SGORR), a program in which high school students visited every sixth grade classroom, three times per year, for a day of activities. The group's activities culminated in a district-wide picnic in the spring. Our leadership team consisted of about a dozen students, with three of us comprising the organizing group.

Zachary had left the school system to pursue his own career, and his good friend and colleague, Marcia Jaffee, became our Staff Advisor. Marcia's guidance included joy, laughter and wisdom, and she deliberately allowed the group to be student-directed. I appreciated her insights around team-building, group process and interpersonal relations. She would remain the SGORR advisor for more than 30 years, and we remain good friends today. I also spent three weeks of my senior year in high school teaching in Marcia's elementary school classroom. Her mentoring and role modeling strongly influenced my decision to pursue a career in education.

As that senior year began, I became the main logistics organizer for SGORR. I had access to the faculty copier, and I'd frequently go to the associate superintendent's office after school to discuss with her the communications needed with elementary school principals and teachers to implement our program.

One part of the curriculum we developed included the documentary *Eye of the Storm*, the story of Iowa elementary schoolteacher Jane Elliott's effort to teach her students about prejudice and racism using eye color as the sorting criteria. It's a powerful story, and Jane Elliott's ongoing work has had a profound impact in the field of diversity training and cultural awareness. For me, her experiment was a lesson in showing how the statements and expectations of people in authority can influence the behavior and self-perception of others. Her teaching has remained a cornerstone of my professional life.

In coordinating that first year of SGORR, I experienced the joys of developing a program, recruiting allies, and implementing an entirely new project that had social relevance. I knew that this sort of creative social entrepreneurship was the type of work I wanted to do with my life.

I moved on to Amherst College, and majored in psychology. I particularly enjoyed social psychology and the studies of Asch, Milgram, Zimbardo, and others whose work indicates the power of social environments on our individual behavior. I spent my senior year researching a thesis on cross-sex friendship, another experience in talking with people about their lives and personal relationships, for which I never ran out of energy. Based on my work with SGORR and this thesis, I graduated from college confident that I could find a career path that would inspire me for the long term.

I spent a lot of time at Amherst off-campus, volunteering in the local community. I organized a project in which Amherst College students volunteered in an after-school program for young children in Holyoke, Massachusetts. These children were mostly Puerto Rican, and the program was located in the run-down mill district of that city. I recruited my friends to join me, and went to Holyoke once or twice per week for about three years. I also volunteered as a tutor in Amherst Regional High School with some Cambodian students. I had just seen the movie *The Killing Fields,* and working with these young refugees helped me connect my life to larger world events.

After leaving Amherst, I made a brief diversion into the field of neuroscience, but within the first few months, I knew that I preferred working with people to working with rats, and that my personality was better suited to a classroom than a laboratory. I attended the Brown University M.A.T. program, which was under the auspices of The Coalition of Essential Schools, a leading school-reform movement based on the writings of Ted Sizer.

At the time, I felt I was in the right place with the right people, and I was excited about becoming a thoughtful teacher and a career school reformer inside the system. The Coalition's principles were progressive and student-centered, and I had a vision that spreading this approach could be a valuable improvement for our society.

Upon completion of that one-year program in 1990, I moved to Washington, D.C., and found a job teaching eighth grade U.S. history in Prince George's County, Maryland. The position was in a rather difficult school with large class sizes, a transient student population, and a handful of hostile students who could create chaos for the vast majority of the teens who wanted a normal school experience. I was in over my head, for sure.

After work, I'd go to a gym with some close friends, and while we were riding our exercise bikes I'd regale them with stories from my day in school. I remember saying things like, "I wish I could just tell the kids who don't want to be there to leave," or, "Forcing them to be in the room just makes it impossible for the rest of us."

These statements were somewhat wistful, selfish impulses of mine, impossible and disconnected from any real solution that I could imagine at that time. I was supposed to connect with these students and persuade them that what I, and the school, had to offer was urgent and important for them. I kept trying.

I felt especially responsible to the serious students in my classes. With more than thirty students per class, mostly I was focused on keeping order. It was hard to hold extended, in-depth conversations or conduct role-plays with those students genuinely curious and ready to participate. I remember offering teens various books and suggestions for learning more outside of my classroom if they desired. The handful of toughest students occupied most of my working time, but I worried even more that I was just wasting the time of many of the other young people.

I remained in the school for a second year, and with the support of the principal, decided to use Alex Haley's book *Roots* as the main curriculum resource for the year. We purchased a paperback copy for every student, and we kept the history textbooks in my classroom for use as needed.

I found the idea inspiring for a school population that was mostly African-American students. However, the ongoing traumas and setbacks in Alex Haley's telling of his family history began to weigh heavily on my students. There weren't many happy days, and by the end of the first semester, the number of students still reading the book had dwindled considerably. Despite it being a self-guided, semi-naïve attempt at curriculum reform, I still recommend the idea with some modifications.

After two years in this school, I was considering moving on from PG County, but then I met Tamara, my wife-to-be. She was then a teacher at another school in the system. She was also ready to move on, but we decided that in just getting to know each other, it made sense to stay in the area for one more year. I transferred to a different middle school, where I encountered one of the best administrators I've known.

His school was considerably calmer than the one I had left, his staff felt more supported and cohesive, and I felt I had some chance at learning the craft of teaching in this environment. The classes I was assigned that year were challenging, but I felt instilled with hope that schools could be safer and more productive than what I had experienced in my first two years as a teacher.

At this point, I still believed that school reform hinged on familiar solutions such as more money to hire better teachers and to provide for smaller class sizes, along with more freedom for teachers to design and implement their own creative curricula. Unfortunately, the state of Maryland was introducing its testing regimen in the mid-1990s, and the general trend of school reform was going in the opposite direction than what I envisioned.

My wife and I then spent a year in Ecuador with a program called WorldTeach. When we returned to the United States, we decided to move to Amherst, Massachusetts. We both landed teaching jobs in the Amherst Regional Public Schools. In 1994, I started once again teaching eighth grade U.S. history, this time at Amherst Regional Junior High School.

The setting was completely new for me as a teacher. Amherst is a college town, home of the University of Massachusetts and the Five-College Consortium that includes Amherst College, Hampshire College, Smith College, and Mt. Holyoke College. Amherst had a well-respected school system with a student population including approximately one-third students of color. The situation was familiar to my own schooling in Shaker Heights, Ohio. I remember thinking, "The school hallways are quieter during class changes here than they were in my old school during classes."

There were plenty of resources and support staff. The community respected and celebrated the school. The staff was generally experienced and professional. At the first staff meeting in September, the principal asked, "How's it going so far?" and I shouted from the back, "I'm in paradise!" My enthusiasm generated some chuckles from other teachers, but I spent that year feeling that finally I had a solid opportunity to develop as a classroom teacher.

I was utilizing resources from Rethinking Schools, an organization that advocates the use of more factually accurate history in the curriculum. I was particularly inspired by Bill Bigelow, a high school teacher who offered workshops through Rethinking Schools. I admired his use of primary resources, role-plays, and writing as the basis for a thoughtful history curriculum.

I also enrolled in a graduate program at the University of Massachusetts School of Education, with the intention of earning an Ed.D. in administration, so that I could become a principal, superintendent, or Secretary of Education one day.

I held the possibility of returning to a more urban school situation, such as those in the nearby cities of Springfield and Holyoke, after gaining more experience and training. For the moment, though, I genuinely felt I was in the right place, and that I was on my way to an interesting and meaningful career to improve public schools.

So...what happened?

I became disillusioned. But this time, I wasn't disillusioned with a particular student, or a class, or a school, or an administrator. I started questioning the educational system itself.

I'd try to inspire students with creative lessons, with limited success. I'd try to scare them into doing their work: "If you don't do these assignments, I'm going to have to give you a bad grade. And if you have a bad grade in eighth grade U.S. history, then..."

However I managed to finish that sentence, whenever I actually listened to myself making these threats, I knew I was being ridiculous. No one's life is genuinely affected by their grades in eighth grade, and I knew it. Inspiring teens to study history and develop some perspective about our world and our place in it is surely a noble and worthy enterprise. I was proud of my teaching. But threatening kids who weren't interested? What was I doing?

I worked hard on my lessons, and spent hours grading papers and giving detailed feedback to my students. I really thought I was making a difference, and in some cases, I did connect personally with kids. But the seriousness with which I took myself also made me impatient and angry with the teens who resisted, or who tried to throw my classes off track.

"What's wrong with these kids, that they come here just to disrupt or distract?" I'd lament. "Can't they just be quiet and play along?"

I owned the failure. It was my fault that these kids, and my previous students in PG County, weren't inspired and engaged. I needed to be more creative, and more responsive. I just had to try harder.

While I struggled with my role as an academic teacher, what really discouraged me was the realization that I was expected to control and punish these students.

"Discipline first!"

"No bathroom passes!"

"Detentions if they are even a second tardy to class!"

"No hats!"

"No gum! Or food or drinks!"

I am not much of an authoritarian, so I am ill-suited to this situation in the first place. But surely, I tried. As I got to know my students and developed relationships, this authoritarian culture of the school weighed on me.

I understood why it existed, and I did appreciate the calm atmosphere of the school that was its primary result. But I felt like I was being forced to be mean, and that if I didn't do so, I was perceived as "un-collegial" or "unprofessional" by the rest of the staff.

I still remember one seemingly trivial moment when a student asked for an extension for a term paper because she had an important skating competition. I was forced to tell both the girl and her mother that I could not accommodate her because of a staff meeting decision to refuse all deadline extensions.

That was not how I wanted to interact with people, and it was not why I had become a teacher. I surely did not believe that her term paper was more important than her skating, and I certainly knew that a one-day delay in her turning it in would affect exactly nobody else but her.

I really had to wonder if I had become trapped into being some sort of prison guard, in pursuit of my academic teaching ambitions.

There was a certain cognitive dissonance between teaching the U.S. history of people fighting for their rights, while I was simultaneously clamping down on students who weren't conforming to the structure.

Really, the school atmosphere felt oppressive to me. I judged it excessively and unnecessarily oppressive. In this well-respected public school, this was how we had to treat kids who generally wanted to come to school every day? I just couldn't reconcile the gap between my image of the school as it ought to be, and my daily reality.

One afternoon, one of my favorite students arrived at my classroom, stood in front of me, and pleaded, "You can't imagine what a waste of time this day has been. Please get me out of here." She was a serious student, a delightful person, and has gone on to earn a Ph.D. in engineering. But that day, I had little to offer her.

"Would you like a pass to the library?" I offered. And then, perhaps more enthusiastically, "Well, my class is about to be awesome. It'll make your day!" I took her statement seriously, and wished I had had a better response to offer her.

Joshua Hornick was another new teacher in 1994. He was teaching eighth grade science. We began to discuss our concerns with each other. He hated seeing teens settle for mediocrity, for identifying the minimum they had to do to get by and get the grade they wanted. He thought teens should be experimenting, risk-taking, soaring. Instead, at school, we were causing them to shut down.

Joshua would exclaim, "Ken, it just drives me crazy. Adolescence should be exciting. These kids have so much energy and so much they could be doing. We're wasting it!"

Joshua is about seven years older than I am. He had been a Wall Street lawyer before he decided to become a teacher. He had also been a peace activist, and had grown up in Manhattan, across the street from John Lennon's home near Central Park.

In addition to being an expert in physics and mathematics, Joshua played the piano and sang. He was reasonably athletic and handsome. He was a renaissance man who also had lots of "notions" about how the world could be different.

He had moved to Amherst as a founding member of a co-housing community, and was more counter-cultural than I was. Joshua would frequently say, "Ken, I have a notion..." and I would roll my eyes to get ready for what was coming next. His notions were always thought-provoking, at least.

Near the end of this first year in Amherst, Joshua and I were discussing ways to improve things at our school. He was the leader of a team making a proposal for a student-centered charter school, modeled after The Sudbury Valley School.

I was underwhelmed. I told him the Massachusetts Charter Commission wasn't interested in this sort of thing, and even if it was, there was no guarantee he'd get a job at this new school as a reward for his efforts. Further, a charter school might be a marginal improvement for the lucky students who win the lottery to attend it, but it would still be full of many of the school-based issues we were questioning.

I was a naysayer, and I more or less ignored this charter application.

Meanwhile, Joshua wanted to tell me about homeschooling. When he was getting his Masters in Education, he had researched how homeschoolers learn science. He had a book he wanted me to read.

I told him to keep his crazy notions to himself; that I was working on a real solution for public schooling, not some homeschooling nonsense.

It wasn't until the following September, in our second year in Amherst, 1995, that I finally accepted his gift of *The Teenage Liberation Handbook: How to Quit School and Get a Real Life and Education,* by Grace Llewellyn.

It was my first introduction to homeschooling. As I have recounted many times, I read it in one sitting and was mesmerized.

Grace was describing a culture I didn't know about: children growing up without attending school, learning what they wanted, under the legal direction of their parents, and turning out fine.

I was flabbergasted, to say the least. Until this point, I was still pretty sure that kids needed to come to schools to find teachers like Joshua and myself, and many of our colleagues who would help them learn what they needed to know, in order to go to college and have a good life.

Grace was challenging that perspective. In fact, she was exposing it. She was forcing me to reconsider some assumptions, and to contemplate the implications if these assumptions were changed.

- What if kids are naturally curious?
- What if we counted the things they are interested in as worthy and valuable?
- What if kids can pursue their strengths as far as they can go?
- Will kids decide to address their weaknesses and gaps when needed?
- What if being happy is more important than being forced to do things that adults believe are "good for you?"
- What if the way we treat kids outside of school is actually more effective in their learning than the way we treat them inside of school?
- What if we had summer camps and after-school activities and sports (...and libraries, YMCAs, youth centers,

camps, sports, tutoring, mentoring) all the time, instead of school?

I was electrified.

Really, this whole school enterprise is unnecessary? Kids learn without school? They go to college without a traditional high school diploma? They become mature, self-aware, entrepreneurial people, without the likes of us teachers? The adult world loves them and welcomes them, even at young ages?

How could this be true and I not know it? Impossible!

By this time, Joshua's charter school application had been denied, and he was considering ways he might support more teens in experimenting with this approach. He hadn't formulated a solid plan yet, but the idea was percolating in his head.

Within a couple of weeks, much to his delight, I barged into his planning.

"Okay," I said, "let's make this real. Let's resign and support all of our students who might be interested in leaving with us!"

5
Getting Started

Ken: So, Joshua, I read The Teenage Liberation
         Handbook. *I have never heard of such a thing.
         I thought homeschooling was parents teaching
         their own kids regular school content at home.
         You know, with textbooks and chalkboards at
         the kitchen table.*

Joshua: *Yes. That's exactly what most people think.*

Ken: *So I'm confused. These "unschoolers" aren't being
         taught by their parents, they aren't necessarily
         learning regular school content, and many of
         them are never at home. What's going on? Is this
         even legal?*

Joshua: *It's legal. Each state has its own legal process. In
         some states, parents have to create a full curricu-
         lum plan of what they intend to teach, while in
         other states they simply have to tell the authori-
         ties of their intention to homeschool.
         Even in the states such as Massachusetts where
         they have to provide a curriculum plan, the states
         can't require that they follow the traditional state
         education curriculum. There are several U.S.
         Supreme Court cases and various state Supreme
         Court cases that have established homeschooling
         as a protected enterprise.*

Ken: *Parents can just file some paperwork and then
         do whatever they want? I'm not sure I agree
         with that.*

Joshua: *If parents are abusive or neglectful, the social workers can intervene. But the state can't force parents to teach any particular content, whether you and I like it or not.*

Ken: *It seems that in many of these families, the parents aren't doing any teaching at all?*

Joshua: *That's true, especially with older kids. It's less true with younger children, where homeschooling parents are likely to be pretty involved. With teens, though, they can have tutors or classes. The homeschoolers have co-ops and other activities that may offer writing, math, science, and all kinds of stuff. That's all fine. There are outdoor survival days, and robotics programs, and 4-H, and Scouts, and martial arts, and all sorts of clubs. Some homeschoolers are busy every day with these sorts of things.*

Ken: *They can just go about their business out in the world? Don't the police question them? Kids are just roaming about at 11:00 in the morning, going to the library? And what if they stop to sit in a coffee shop? Isn't there some sort of truancy?*

Joshua: *No, Ken, homeschoolers aren't being arrested for truancy. Homeschooling is a legitimate way to fulfill the requirements for compulsory schooling, so the kids aren't truant. They can go about their business freely and explain to anyone inquiring that they are homeschoolers.*
Consider it this way: Homeschoolers out and about in the coffee shop at 11:00 a.m. are no different from school kids out and about at 3:00 p.m. after school.

Most young homeschoolers don't wander about without their parents, but teens certainly can do so. It's great. It's part of their learning, actually.

Ken: *So, these parents are working while their kids are going from class to class, and hanging out in the library and coffee shops? And the kids are learning math with tutors, or on their own? This all seems a bit preposterous to me.*

Joshua: *Ken, stop it. What do you think happens every day after school, when the middle school and high school let out at 2:30? What happens in the summer, for kids who have working parents? People make arrangements. The modern homeschooling movement has been going on for twenty years. Grace isn't making this up. You just don't know about it.*

Ken: *And they can sign up for community college at age 15 or 16? Or audit courses at private colleges? And they can apply and get accepted to elite schools?*

Joshua: *They can and they do. Go ask your people at Amherst College. In fact, some people argue that these homeschoolers and unschoolers are even more ready for college than regular high school graduates.*

Ken: *So...wait! These people live free and interesting lives as kids. They can be out in the community with jobs, volunteer work, and classes. They have tutors and groups. They can go to college. And if there are enough of them, they can even have a social life of some sort? It seems to me like this is some kind of cheating. They are having their cake and eating it, too. This doesn't seem fair to me.*

Joshua: Yes, that's all true. But you should know, home-schooling is not really an elitist or separatist movement. Many homeschoolers are low-income, and are living a pretty frugal lifestyle. They are doing it because they want a better family life and more immediate freedom for their children to be engaged in the world.

Ken: Homeschooling isn't just a bunch of conservatives withdrawing from school to isolate their children from the mainstream? I'm still dubious about this.

Joshua: It's true that conservatives have been part of modern homeschooling from the beginning. However, there have always been many different groups involved, even if this hasn't been portrayed well in the media.
The homeschooling movement now has become much more diverse, and it's growing rapidly. In fact, homeschooling is growing much faster than private schooling now, and it's impossible to label everyone. People are seeking better options for their children, and sometimes homeschooling is more appealing than any school they can find.

Ken: I'm not done with you, yet! I've got a lot more research to do before I believe you. But two questions:
1) If you are so certain about this homeschooling thing, what are you doing working here? You need to be out there with those homeschoolers.
2) If this is all true, why aren't more people doing it? If it's all so glorious and wonderful, why is everyone still going to school?

This conversation took place in September, 1995. Within a week or two, those final questions were reframed with these additions: "Joshua, I'm leaving with you!" and "Let's make this approach possible for all of our current students who would be interested and ready to try this approach."

I had quickly come to see that there were very few teen homeschoolers in our area, and that Joshua and I could not earn a living by being their teachers. I also realized that these existing homeschoolers were not really our target audience.

We wanted to improve the lives of the students we had been teaching in the junior high school. Our goal was to take this understanding of self-directed learning and make this approach an exciting way to improve all of our lives.

I started reading a series of books about homeschooling, including John Holt's books such as *How Children Fail, How Children Learn,* and *Teach Your Own.* I read the homeschooling classic of that era, *Homeschooling for Excellence,* by Micki and David Colfax. My favorite homeschooling book turned out to be *Family Matters: Why Homeschooling Makes Sense* by David Guterson, author of the best-selling novel, *Snow Falling on Cedars.*

Guterson, a high school English teacher at the time, describes his family decision to utilize homeschooling for his own children. His sharing of many discussions and concerns involved in this process resonated deeply with me.

I also read *Punished by Rewards* by Alfie Kohn, which reports the evidence in social psychology about the harm of grades, money, and praise on intrinsic motivation. This book, after Grace Llewellyn's *Teenage Liberation Handbook,* has had the strongest impact on my adult life.

Along the way, Joshua passed along his copy of John Taylor Gatto's *Dumbing Us Down: The Hidden Curriculum of Compulsory Schooling,* and I was thrilled to see Gatto's critiques of the school system.

I was still involved in my Ed.D. courses at the University of Massachusetts, and I arranged for an independent study about college admissions for homeschoolers.

I wrote to one hundred college admissions offices (two in each state, a major public state university and a small liberal arts college) to find out how many homeschoolers were applying, how many were being accepted, and how that ratio compared to overall admissions rates.

While the number of responses was small, and the number of homeschooling applicants was tiny in comparison to total applicants, my limited conclusion was that each college had a process for admitting homeschoolers, and that their admission rates seemed to be more or less the same as the overall rates.

In another class, I designed a research paper for which I interviewed the seven local teen unschooolers I could find, and tried to assess their experiences in comparison to those of traditional students.

I remember thinking that these teens were self-aware, articulate, and reasonably knowledgeable. They were quirky, perhaps, but interesting. It seemed to me that they weren't "behind in academics" or "isolated from society" or "excluded from opportunities," compared to the overall set of teens I was teaching in school.

I was learning that yes, indeed, this homeschooling world and the subculture of unschooling were valid lifestyles I simply hadn't known about. I was uncovering a secret that most people didn't know existed. What's more, Joshua and I were going to spread this information and, by our own efforts, make it accessible to mainstream families.

This felt tremendously revolutionary and exciting. We were going to make school optional for everyone! As we turned the idea over and over, and reviewed it from various angles, we couldn't see any obstacles or any flaws. Sure, no one else was doing this, and we'd have to make it up as we went along, but that was part of the adventure.

It would be legal, right? I remember reading homeschooling laws in various states, and even speaking with lawyers who had been involved in some homeschooling cases. Over and over again, we came to the conclusion that our vision was well within the legal bounds of homeschooling in Massachusetts.

I still clearly remember my first extended conversation with a skeptic. I know it was in late October, 1995, because I was watching my hometown Cleveland Indians play in the World Series, while at a special celebration of my wife's family in Maine.

One of my wife's cousins, Marcus, was an academically oriented high school student who would go on to graduate from Dartmouth College. He and I spent the entirety of that night's baseball game arguing the pros and cons of supporting teenagers in leaving school and embarking on self-directed learning.

Marcus could see how academically curious and inspired kids might benefit, but he was concerned for teens who might choose to "sit and do nothing."

He heard my views about how being a teacher that assigned these students work they didn't want to do was not working, and we went back and forth for hours. By the end of the night, Marcus conceded something along the lines of, "I get it. I see how this could be good for some teens."

I don't think I won his full, ringing endorsement that evening, but over the years, his parents have become very enthusiastic North Star loyalists.

At Thanksgiving, 1995, I went home to Cleveland with my wife, and told my parents that I would be resigning my teaching position at the end of the academic year to start this project.

My parents had very little connection with the word "homeschooling," and had difficulty grasping the full vision of what I had in mind. Nevertheless, they were immediately one hundred percent supportive. I come from a family of entrepreneurs, and they were thrilled that I was leaving the bureaucracy of schooling to "start my own business."

They did understand that I was starting something unique, that it wasn't exactly an "alternative school," and they celebrated the notion with joy.

They have remained steadfast and generous in their support, both emotional and financial, to the present. They have become experts in self-directed learning, as well, and they now recommend the approach to many of their friends whose grandchildren are not satisfied with their school experiences.

During the rest of that academic year, I carried some irrational fear that if the school authorities understood our intentions of helping currently enrolled students to utilize homeschooling, they might try to discredit us before we could get started.

I knew for sure that there was no basis in reality for this concern, and that our colleagues would respond to our vision with skepticism, amusement, or neutrality.

One major step in dispelling my worries was our decision to meet directly with our superintendent, Dr. Gus Sayer. He had hired both Joshua and me just two years earlier, and we had good relationships with him.

In addition to giving him the heads-up about our impending resignations, we asked him to make us experts in writing homeschooling plans.

What was he looking for from parents who were planning to homeschool? How could we help our future students and their parents present solid plans that would make this process conflict-free?

Dr. Sayer responded more with concern for our well-being than with any objection to the idea, and he offered us other positions that might allow us to find a happier niche working in the school system.

He then proceeded to explain his reactions to the homeschooling plans he had seen in the last few years, and we gained some beneficial clarity about his point of view.

This meeting has turned out to be profoundly helpful, as we have experienced almost no conflicts with any local superintendents in all of our years. The meeting also further confirmed for us that what we wanted to do would be legal and logically possible, however strange it sounded to others.

Dr. Sayer's concerns were mainly that we would never be able to earn a living comparable to that of public school teachers and administrators. He was correct. Joshua and I were prepared for a year or so of very low "start-up" salaries, but we hoped to be earning a more reasonable salary by year three, at the latest.

To this end, we knew we would establish our program as a non-profit organization that could accept donations and conduct fundraisers. We knew that many of our target public school-attending students would not be able to afford to pay much to our enterprise, let alone full private school tuition. We drafted a budget, and we began the process of recruiting potential members for our Board of Directors.

I have since learned that many entrepreneurs reject the non-profit model because it means surrendering some self-control to an external group of people. I confess to never having any hesitations or concerns along these lines. Joshua and I were recruiting friends, neighbors, and allies who agreed with the goal of providing an innovative alternative-to-school for all interested families, and the idea of some bad outcome just never occurred to me.

As the spring moved along, we had a number of people who were involved with youth, education, or social justice that wanted to be involved.

One of Joshua's contacts was a successful homeschooling parent, T.R. Rosenberg, who happened to have an education and a counseling-related non-profit corporation that was then inactive.

T.R. and his family had no immediate plans for this non-profit, and he agreed to "adopt" us as a project of his Pathfinder Foundation. With this stroke of kindness, Pathfinder Learning Center was born.

The legal "directors" were T.R. and his Pathfinder Foundation directors, and our "Board of Trustees" was composed of friends, who would become our active supporters and workers. (This situation would remain in place for six years.)

One of T.R.'s lasting impacts was that he coined the phrase "Liberated Learners" as the title for Pathfinder's newsletter in 1998. That phrase also became the name of the organization we created in 2013 for our consulting work.

We held our first Board of Trustees meetings during the spring of 1996, identifying people and organizations who might refer teens or be interested in collaborating with us on activities and programs. We reviewed the budget and discussed fundraising and outreach events. Our sense of challenging the system continued to grow.

We knew that, because of our commitment to this process, every family could have the power of opting out of school. We could welcome students from any nearby school, public or private. What if everyone wanted to do so? We could imagine the possibility of a massive walkout from schools, however unlikely. This idea of making self-directed learning understood, accessible, and appealing was powerful, indeed.

During the last week of school in June, 1996, we went public. We announced our first public meeting to be held the following week, and we mailed out invitations to many of our former students. We lined up three veteran "unschooling" people to share their experiences. To our delight, more than eighty people attended that first meeting.

The stories from Kyle Homstead, Raina Askew, and Ana Brady-Smith became the first of our many panel presentations, in which teens describe how their choice to leave school was the most pivotal and powerful moment of their lives. They were living full, active lives at ages 13-18, instead of waiting to graduate from high school, and they found every avenue of college study and employment open to them.

Kyle, in his mid-twenties, was a successfully self-employed sound engineer, who had unschooled in his teen years and gained a head start on his career. Raina was a former student of Joshua's, whom he had supported to use homeschooling during this planning year, much to her and her mother's delight. Ana was a younger, long-term unschooler, who exuded confidence and self-direction for her many interests.

These three young people described feeling energized,

happy, and engaged with others. After their stories, Joshua and I explained how we wanted to help the people in the audience be like our presenters. It was a compelling presentation.

By late summer, we had twenty-five teens enrolled at Pathfinder. Some were our former students: Willow Hersh, Ramon Elinevsky, Tibet Sprague, Jacob Abernethy, Raf Anzovin, Lesley Arak.

Some were local homeschoolers, curious to see what our program might offer them. Some were complete strangers, who had heard about Pathfinder and thought it sounded great. I went to the homes of some prospective members that summer, sharing the vision with worried parents and teens, one family at a time.

Our first payment came from the family of Rene Rives, a student from our former school, whom I had not known. I can still remember holding that first check and making that first deposit. These people were signing on!

The adventure was beginning.

In July, 1996, we rented a small, three-room office in downtown Amherst, almost in the shadow of the high school. We moved in our used furniture and books. We were ready to go.

North Star Philosophy – Basic Guiding Principles

1.   **Young people want to learn.** Human beings are learning creatures. We don't have to persuade babies to be curious or to seek competence and understanding. The same can be true of teenagers. Rather than trying to motivate teenagers, we support their basic human drive to learn and grow. Where obstacles—internal or external—have gotten in the way of this intrinsic drive, we focus on helping teenagers overcome or remove these obstacles.

2. **Learning happens everywhere, not just in school settings.** Conventional wisdom says that children "go to school to learn," as though learning can only occur in places specially designed for that purpose. We believe that people learn all the time and in all kinds of places. It doesn't have to look like school or feel like school to be valuable, and it's not necessary to make distinctions between "schoolwork" and "your own hobbies" or "for credit" and "not for credit." As one teenager who had recently left school observed, "Everything I do counts now."

3. **It really is okay to quit school.** Many young people who are miserable in school—academically or socially—stay because they believe that quitting school will rule out (or at least diminish) the possibility of a successful future. We believe that young people can achieve a meaningful and successful adulthood without going to school. We've seen it happen, over and over again.

4. **How people behave under one set of circumstances and assumptions does not predict how they will behave under a very different set of circumstances and assumptions.** School success or failure is not necessarily a predictor of a child's potential for success or failure outside of school. An unmotivated student may become enthusiastic and committed after she's left school. A student who doesn't thrive in a classroom environment may become successful when allowed to learn through apprenticeships or in one-on-one tutorials. When we change the approach, the structure, and the assumptions, all kinds of other changes often follow.

5. **Structure communicates as powerfully as words, and often more powerfully.** It's ineffective and disingenuous to tell kids that we want them to be self-motivated, or that we want them to value learning for its own sake, when the structure of their lives and their educations is actually communicating the opposite message. Voluntary (rather than compulsory) classes, the ability to choose what one studies rather than following a required curriculum, and the absence of tests and grades all contribute to a structure that supports and facilitates intrinsic motivation and self-directed learning.

6. **As adults working with young people, we should mostly strive to "make possible" rather than "make sure."** Most of the time, we can't truly make sure that young people learn any particular thing; learning just doesn't work that way. A group of adults can decide that all fifth-graders should learn fractions, but when it comes to each individual child's genuine understanding and retention, we can't actually make it happen or guarantee that it will happen if they're not yet ready. As adults, what we can do is try to make things possible for young people: Provide access, offer opportunity, figure out what kind of support will be most helpful, do whatever we can to help navigate the challenges and problems that arise.

7. **The best preparation for a meaningful and productive future is a meaningful and productive present.** Too often, education is thought of in terms of preparation: "Do this now, even if it doesn't feel connected to your most pressing interests and concerns, because later on you'll

find it useful." We believe that helping teenagers to figure out what seems interesting and worth doing right now, in their current lives, is also the best way to help them develop self-knowledge and experience at figuring out what kind of life they want and what they need to do or learn in order to create that life. In other words, it's the best preparation for their futures.

– Drafted by Susannah Sheffer

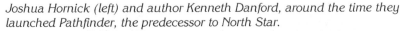

Joshua Hornick (left) and author Kenneth Danford, around the time they launched Pathfinder, the predecessor to North Star.

6

The Model

The final act of my public school teaching career in June, 1996, encapsulated many of the frustrations I had at that time with being a teacher. In lieu of a final exam, I assigned a final project, for which students had to interview a relative or neighbor about their involvement with or relationship to a recent historical event we had studied in U.S. history class.

It could be about a military experience, or race relations, or involvement in local affairs...or anything, really. The project required students to provide some background information about the historical event, compose a list of questions they developed to ask their interviewee, write a brief biography of their person, include a general description of the answers, and offer some summary of what the student learned from doing this interview.

Students turned in these interviews the last day of class. During exam week, I carefully read each paper and wrote long notes back to each student. I expected the students to come pick up these interviews on the last day of school, when they came to get their report cards. I also hoped they would take these interviews home to share with their families, and perhaps even to save them as a worthwhile project.

Alas, on that last day, only a handful of students came by my room to pick up their projects. Several of those students just flipped to the back page to see what grade I had assigned it, and then, without reading the comments I had written, dropped it in the trash can. To say I was heartsick puts it mildly. At the end of the day,

I stared at the stack of two-thirds of the projects that remained. I left them on my desk for the next day or so while I cleaned my room. By the end of the week, I had to pick them up and put them all in the recycling bin with my own hands.

That was a long time ago, but I still flinch when I remember that moment. Unfortunately, that moment was more of an exclamation point on my teaching career rather than a unique occurrence. For the past six years, I had been judging myself on whether I could get students to complete my agenda with sincere effort.

Joshua and I were now walking away from that responsibility. We were going to start asking students what they wanted to accomplish, rather than assign them tasks. We were going to encourage them to practice self-evaluation of their progress, rather than rely on our narrow grade assessments of their tangible work.

We were going to ask teens where and with whom they wanted to spend their time, rather than require that they be in our space, attending our activities. We were intending to support them in moving on to college, work, and other opportunities, when they felt ready for their next phase of life, rather than insist they complete our agenda to receive a diploma.

Also, we would never again be in position to give or withhold a bathroom pass, assign a detention, or hassle students about their trivial wardrobe choices.

In truth, we wanted to surrender all of the arbitrary authority that is vested in teachers by the system of schooling, and rely on our natural authority of being decent and useful adults to form the basis of our relationships with students. Skeptics have often called this type of vision irresponsible, indulgent, and misguided, but we saw it as empowering, respectful, and challenging.

By this time, my research into homeschooling had convinced me that my goals were aligning: The things I didn't want to do weren't necessary for learning, and the things I did want to do were possible through homeschooling.

While we felt revolutionary in terms of school reform, we saw our intentions as both realistic and familiar. We felt we were being realistic, given the success of existing homeschoolers and unschoolers who were thriving. We knew that school achievement does not correlate with adult success in terms of income, happiness, or any other measure. We were questioning a social norm, but all around us, reality suggested that we were on solid ground.

Also, our preferred terms for working with teens were familiar. Outside of schooling, our vision was normal: Many of our students were involved with teams, lessons, clubs, and hobbies outside of school, which they chose for themselves and pursued on their own terms. Most adults we knew belonged to various health clubs, civic groups, and religious organizations that operate with these assumptions about respecting people's choices.

We had students who held jobs, possessed strong work ethics, and understood what it meant to honor agreements. We believed we could expand these sorts of relationships to academic learning and life in general for teens.

There was another way that I knew that our "revolutionary" vision was "realistic and familiar." The values of interacting with people on these terms had been instilled in me, without thought or discussion, for my entire life. In retrospect, I can now see clearly that my primary role models for my work at North Star have been my parents, Peter and Susan Danford.

During the first years of my teaching career, I tried to describe my experiences to my parents. They listened, but they couldn't fully empathize with the challenges I was facing in my classroom. It finally dawned on me why: They didn't have any experience of trying to manage a captive audience.

My father has owned his jewelry store since 1973. My mother immediately became his bookkeeper, despite having no formal training in the field, making her a fine role model for self-directed learning.

One day, when I was describing the sorts of problems I was encountering in my classroom, I realized, "My
parents only deal with people who choose to come into
their store! They basically make people happy by selling
them wedding rings and birthday gifts. The store is a happy
place, because people enjoy going there to accomplish
something important to them."

I had never considered the jewelry store from this
perspective before, and I was stunned at the realization.

"That's what I want to do! Teach history to people
who want to learn it. I want to host a space where people
are happy to enter, where they come because they have a
purpose in mind for themselves."

I wanted to work in a setting like my father's store.
I wanted to "retail" education. Hmmm...for a fellow who
had pretty much rejected the idea of going into the family
business, this was quite a shock.

I did not romanticize the time, effort, and risk involved
in my parent's work. My father worked six days per week
when I was young, and my mother spent many hours doing
the bookkeeping. She did her work at home, which meant
the boundaries between the store and home were blurry.
After dinner, she might sit at her desk and ask my father
questions about the business. I also heard their normal
complaints and frustrations.

But, one thing was clear: My father enjoyed going to
work every day. He didn't argue with people about using
the bathroom in his store, or being late for an appointment,
or wearing hats inside his store. He didn't have people
come into his store who had no intention or desire to be
there. He did not try to convince people to buy things they
did not want.

Everything was different; upside-down, or reversed
from what I was trying to do with my students as an eighth
grade U.S. history teacher.

Today, my main image of the store continues to
be walking in the door and seeing my father behind the
counter, working with a customer. With some amusement,

satisfaction, and perhaps irony, it's a scene familiar at North Star, when my own children walk in the door and see me in a meeting.

However, back in the early 1990s, when I first had the thought that I wanted to relate to my students the way my dad relates to his customers, I had no idea how to make that happen. It was a fleeting notion, a pipe dream. I didn't really consider quitting my teaching career to work in summer camps, after-school programs, or other youth work.

I just carried on with my career, holding this concept as a subtle insight about my critique of schooling. I had no way back then to imagine that I would find a way to achieve this vision.

The Model

So what was the actual way? What would the thing be that we were creating, to work with kids on our own terms? We didn't have a model to replicate. As I mentioned in Chapter 1, Joshua had been interested in the Sudbury Valley School, a day school based on the famous English boarding school, Summerhill, founded by A.S. Neill.

Sudbury is a private school, where students have no requirements, and where decisions are made democratically by the full community of students and staff. In fact, beyond Sudbury, there was a movement of democratic free schools including the Albany Free School, which were the survivors or descendants of an open-school reform movement of the 1960s and 1970s.

I did find the people and the ideas of these schools inspiring, particularly their commitment to trusting children and respecting their choices. However, these were still schools that required attendance five hours per day, five days per week, 180 days per year. They offered diplomas upon graduation, encouraging students to attend through age 18.

I saw these models as a different form of schooling; compelling in a certain way, but not an alternative to school. Joshua and I were heading in a different direction.

At this same time, we saw that many homeschoolers organized sophisticated co-ops, full of classes, activities, and socializing. I was impressed with what I saw in my local community and read about around the country. Nevertheless, I saw that these programs weren't what we had in mind.

These homeschooling co-ops gathered for specific classes in libraries, community centers, churches, and other spaces available on a temporary basis, and did not have permanent spaces. They were low-cost, do-it-yourself communities that did not have full-time staff earning a living by organizing or teaching. They often required parents to remain present with their children.

In short, these co-ops were focused on providing activities for people who had already made the commitment to homeschooling. They were not focused on making homeschooling work for children and families feeling trapped in school, but lacking all of the resources needed to utilize homeschooling.

We wanted to help our former school students leave school with us, which was fundamentally a different goal from what most homeschooling co-ops entertain.

I remain thrilled and inspired by the expanse of offerings that local homeschoolers create for themselves and others, a topic I will return to in the concluding chapter of this book.

The model that made the most sense to us was that of community center. We saw membership clubs such as the YMCA or health clubs as the right direction.

These are places where members can go as much or as little as they wish, to do the activities that appeal to them. They offer space, equipment, and a sense of community for everyone. They offer a schedule of specific classes and individual trainers for people interested in such guidance. There are no grades, certificates, or requirements.

This description also fits many senior centers, Boys and Girls Clubs, and—though I was once loathe to mention it—country clubs.

Both of my grandmothers and my parents were active participants at their private country clubs when I was young. I did not feel comfortable with the exclusive nature of these places, but I saw my family members deriving great use and pleasure from these communities.

Years later, I was reading Pat Farenga's revised version of John Holt's book *Teach Your Own: The John Holt Book of Homeschooling,* and I nearly fell out of my chair when I read the following passage (pp. 119-120):

> *In some ways, the country clubs that rich folks belong to are a much better model of what we want than a school. Take away the eighteen-hole golf courses, the elaborate tennis courts and other facilities, the palatial clubhouse, and what's left is very close in spirit to what we are after. You don't have to play golf just because you go to the golf club. You don't have to do anything. There are certain kinds of resources there for you to use, if you want, but you can spend the day there sitting in a chair and looking at the sky. Why not an inexpensive version of the same thing? A country club without the country—or perhaps a different kind of country, just a little patch of field or woods or whatever is handy. If we can keep the idea of a family club in mind, we will probably make more sensible choices and decisions.*

There you have it. Family is destiny. The jewelry store and the country club turned out to be the models for my adult life.

There are plenty of other institutions that come close to our vision, but aren't quite there. My children loved their summer camp experiences, and as young adults both continue to work in the field of camps during the summer. I value these places immensely, and once wrote a blog piece about comparing camps and schools for the *Huffington Post*: "We Love Camp! Can We Love School?"

The fact that camp has some absolute requirements pulls it a bit away from the model I wanted to create. The same analysis goes for many sports and after-school programs that children love. In creating an alternative to school, I wanted to create the most freedom possible for teens to set their own goals and to impose as little as possible of my own judgment and preferences.

Sometimes we compare ourselves to my favorite American institution, the public library. Libraries have lots of available resources, and librarians are available to help as requested. Somehow they manage to keep a straight face and their comments to themselves when they see we are only checking out videos or potentially embarrassing books.

Basically, Joshua and I wanted to be hosts of a club, with the non-judgmental behavior of the finest librarian. This vision merged our interests and personalities with an accurate estimate of what most of our eighth grade students needed, to leave the junior high school and embark on self-directed learning. Perhaps it's not surprising that many North Star alumni have gone into the library field.

Joshua and I began the process of designing our program with the realization that, for the most part, our junior high school students accepted the cultural premise that they needed to go to school, and they weren't going to throw their futures away. They had friends at school, as well as some worthwhile sports, clubs, and activities. How would homeschooling be better?

Many of our students had single parents, or two working parents, with no one easily available to provide support or transportation. Also, many of these families did not feel confident about opting out of what they saw as mainstream culture and expectations. Their primary goal was helping their children complete high school, not be part of some experiment in alternative education.

These issues were separate from the practical concerns about the costs of our program, and whether a family could afford to pay the membership fees. We knew immediately that coaching teens and families to consider an alternative to school was going to be a hard sell, but we were undeterred. Inspired by the movie *Field of Dreams*, we were confident that, "If we build it, they will come!"

Informed by this sense of a "club," we identified the specific services we felt we had to offer to help any teen have a viable, appealing, and sustainable alternative to school.

Full support and explanation of the legal homeschooling process and self-directed learning, as an approach different from schooling

We explained that homeschooling does not have to mean replicating school at home, nor does it require that parents teach their children. It does mean, in Massachusetts, that the parents must provide their local school superintendent with a curriculum plan of what they have in mind for English, Math, History, Science, and some electives, along with likely books, materials, and other resources they expect to offer their child.

We gave parents a template to use for writing this document, and we reviewed their specific plans before they submitted them to their local superintendent. In addition to this legal homeschooling process, we brainstormed a range of ideas and goals for what the teen most wanted to learn and what concerns or other needs existed for the parents so that everyone could feel good about the outcome. We also gave each new member a copy of *The Teenage Liberation Handbook*.

In these meetings, Joshua and I discovered that we were really in the business of liberating people from all kinds of fears. Parents were worried that they could get in trouble if their children didn't do enough school-like work. We had to help them understand that there really were no homeschooling police investigating them, and that as long as they communicated effectively with the school system, there was little risk of trouble.

Sometimes, teens struggled to accept freedom, even within familiar school terms: "Can I really read any books

I want? For math, could I work on real-life things like a budget or how taxes work?" My favorite question of all time was, "If I join Pathfinder, can I study both Spanish and French?" I remember trying to keep a straight face and responding, "Do you think I could stop you from studying more than one language?"

Really, this child had never considered that they could learn something taught in school without permission.

Outside of academics, the same thing occurred with teens interested in the arts, or music, or entrepreneurship. "You mean, we can start with the major interests first, and then do the academics whenever we want?"

We were offering a serious challenge to everyone's assumptions about how things work in the world.

Fairly early on in our work, Joshua devised a worksheet to ask about interests in a variety of fields, with academic interests being just one of ten. Some of the other topics we asked teens to consider whether they had any interests in were: hands-on projects, sports and exercise, music and art, money-making, social opportunities, private time, religious activities, and family time.

We discovered that many parents and teens found it difficult to see their own hobbies as "counting" for part of a homeschooling plan or even towards building a meaningful life. "I just do puzzles for fun," was a way of discounting completing intricate jigsaws with the family, volunteering at a senior center program, or organizing events at a local gaming store.

"Yes, that counts!" became part of our refrain. As many of us understand, these informal activities often lead to jobs or careers. Even if they do not, they are valuable in their own right, and there is simply no reason to discount any activity that gives us joy and challenge.

One hard part of these conversations was teens who, when asked about their interests, just shrugged their shoulders.

"I don't know," they would mumble, avoiding eye contact. In many cases, these young people were genuinely unsure about what to say. They did not like reading books for fun, they had never felt inspired by a class in school, and they really didn't know how to respond to a person like me asking them about their interests.

I would sometimes ask questions such as, "How do you spend your time on the weekends? What did you do last summer?" with little success. The most memorable of these conversations came a few years into our work with one student, Tessa Morrissey.

When I pressed her about having no interests, she looked at me, a bit exasperated, and said, "I told you, I don't know what I do for fun. I just hate school. I mean, when I'm with my friends, that's what we do: We hate school together. That's our activity, hating school."

We aimed to conclude these meetings with two overlapping agreements. One was the legal homeschooling agreement that the parents would submit to their local schools, and the other was a more holistic agreement between the students and their parents about their priorities and visions for the coming months.

This process was very different from how we had been interacting with students and parents as schoolteachers, and we reveled in the flexibility we had created for all of us.

A calendar of classes and activities, including traditional academic subjects as well as the arts, music, and other, more unusual topics

While we were not trying to replicate school, we wanted to offer some weekly classes for two reasons. First, we were teachers, and we wanted to continue sharing our knowledge and skills with teens. I wanted to teach Social Issues, U.S. History, Psychology, Popular Economics, and Media Literacy. Joshua wanted to teach Building Model Rockets, Electricity, Fourier Mathematics, and much more. He wanted to put on a theater show and direct a jazz ensemble. We both had plenty of ideas for trips and community involvement.

Second, we wanted to offer a calendar of classes to reassure potential students and parents that they would not have to create everything for themselves from scratch. Most people found the idea of living without school to be daunting, and we needed to make it feel manageable. One step in that direction was to establish a calendar of activities that our members could join.

Very quickly, we had a number of volunteers offering classes as well. One of the highlights of this process was realizing just how many adults were interested in sharing their expertise with interested teens, even as a volunteer. Soon we had friends, college students, and general community members approaching us about offering a class. Some of the parents of our teen members wanted to contribute their time, as well.

When people asked, "What would you like me to teach? What do you need at North Star?" We replied, "What's the one thing you have learned that you wish had been offered when you were fourteen years old?" or "What's the one topic you feel most excited about sharing with others?"

Before long, we had a book group, a writing workshop, logic, herbalism, and all sorts of activities on the calendar. It felt to me like the fable, *Stone Soup*. We built the fire, filled a pot with water, and threw in a few starter items. Before long, we had a pretty hearty stew.

While these classes were ungraded and frequently had little or no homework, they were serious endeavors. Every class seemed to be somebody's favorite activity of the week. When this was not the case, poorly attended classes were removed from the calendar (including my own), and we asked the teacher to try something else or to come back another time to try again.

Tutoring for teens interested in specific subjects

Joshua and I loved the opportunity to work with students one-on-one. I imagine most teachers share this feeling. Unfortunately, the moments in school to have one-on-one interactions are limited. Sometimes, students demonstrated enthusiastic interest in a topic we were studying, and I would offer them an extra book to read or documentary to watch. The response was usually, "No, thank you. I have way too much to do already."

Now, in our new program, we could respond to a student's interest with an offer for a one-on-one tutorial. We started with several in traditional topics, such as algebra, and test preparation for the GED or SATs. However, we could also suggest a novel, or a movie, or an article to an individual student, and proceed on a private basis.

I had several history tutorials, and one that has stuck with me was with Steve Theberge. He was seventeen years old, and a political activist. He was a member of a local group called the Revolutionary Anarchist Youth, and he wanted to study anarchism. We read a number of books on the topic, and tried to sort out some of the specifics. Steve was reading Howard Zinn's book, *A People's History of the United States,* and he wanted to know more about recent conflicts between minority groups and the United States government.

We learned about the conflict in Waco, Texas with the Branch Davidians, and then researched the MOVE bombing in Philadelphia. These projects required trips to the library at the University of Massachusetts to get materials that weren't available elsewhere, and the trip to the W.E.B. Dubois Library was itself fascinating for us. Clearly, this interaction was very different from anything I could have done with Steve if I had been his high school history teacher.

Steve and I also had a math tutorial to help him prepare for his SATs. The outcome was not particularly successful, but even with his poor math scores, Steve was admitted to Columbia University.

(To complete his story, Steve had a competing interest with his political inclinations, which was pottery. After North Star, in addition to graduating from Columbia, he completed a two-year pottery apprenticeship. He also worked for the War Resister's League in New York City, and spent three years living as a monk at a Buddhist monastery in Japan. As an adult, he has chosen to focus on his pottery, and he is now a professional potter in Northampton, Massachusetts.)

Joshua was pursuing high-level physics and calculus, reading philosophy books, and offering one-on-one music lessons with individual members. As we ramped up the program, some of our volunteers were willing to meet with our members privately, as well.

Many teens found it difficult to ask for tutoring. They hadn't ever contemplated doing something on their own with a teacher before. Tutorials had a connotation of being for teens at the ends of the academic spectrum: either remedial in nature, for youth struggling with basic skills, or nerdy pursuits for the "smart" kids. One-on-ones were a new concept for teens who had been muddling through school, drawing little attention to themselves.

These tutorials were a service Joshua and I enjoyed providing to our members. They were relatively few in number and took up a relatively small amount of our time. They were a good way to develop relationships and get to know our members better, and provided a sense of accomplishment for the teens.

Now, North Star offers thirty to fifty one-on-one meetings per day, and tutorials are one of the central aspects of our program. While algebra and traditional math remain the most common topic for tutorials, they include many other interests, such as going for a walk to identify trees, or learning to make sushi in our kitchen. Many involve writing, music, art, foreign languages, and computer programming.

The tutors include our Core Staff, local college students, alumni, friends, parents of current members, and even teens themselves. It turns out that many people prefer to learn certain types of things in a one-on-one setting, and our model supports that approach with a type of breadth, depth, and flexibility that is different from what schools can offer.

An easily-accessible, safe, and comfortable gathering space that is open during the day

Joshua and I knew immediately that we would have to secure an office space where teens could hang out and spend time with each other. We needed a center that was conveniently located, where teens could come and go independently, either by foot or public transportation. We didn't want to have teens "stuck" at our center waiting for rides with no other way to get on with their days. We also wanted teens to have access to a library, stores, food, and organizations that might offer internships or volunteer opportunities.

In the summer of 1996, we rented a three-room office suite in a small, house-like building in downtown Amherst. We shared the building with our realtor landlords, along with a lawyer, a therapist, an investment advisor, and another youth service program's office. As our population grew that first year, we were able to use some finished rooms in the basement as well, and in the summer of 1997, we converted the basement garage space into an open community room.

We remained in that basement suite of five rooms for six years, as we had low rent in a central location. It was a bit low-ceilinged and musty, and felt like the scrappy office of an upstart movement. Sometimes I would cringe showing it to newcomers, and say, "Remember, it's not all about the space. It's about the idea of helping kids to live a different lifestyle!" In my current consulting work, I encourage people to start in offices more akin to our second space: a well-lit, above-ground, professional office space we moved to in 2002.

We are now in our fourth location, and the priorities have stayed constant: A space that is independently accessible for teens with places to walk to nearby. We also have always had some available yard or grassy play space. Inside, we have at least one large Common Room and a series of smaller rooms, for small groups and tutorials. We now fully occupy a 4,800-square-foot office building in Sunderland,

Massachusetts, allowing us to have classes such as a Rock Band and Theatre, without disturbing any co-tenants.

The physical characteristics of the center are worth noting, but the most important aspect of the space is our ability to host a safe and welcoming place for teens to hang out.

It turns out that the world does not offer many such spaces to teenagers. There is precious little freedom to hang out in school. Many after-school activities and sports have relatively little downtime for teens to socialize. Libraries are quiet spaces. It turned out that our intention to provide a space for teens to socialize during the day was actually more novel than we realized. And, it was more important than we had imagined.

From day one, we considered the opportunity to socialize in our Common Room as important as any of the other services we provided. Many of our members craved time to talk, compare stories, or simply listen to others. Some wanted to play games together.

We frequently had new members whose main priority was making new friends or developing their social skills. They wanted to know everybody's name, and they liked to know everything that was going on at the center. They had never had the chance to simply sit, observe, and chat informally before, and this opportunity was more compelling and urgent than was attending any particular class.

In addition to the Common Room, we set up a Library as a quiet room, for those who wanted to escape the stimulation and commotion of the larger group. We made other rooms available for teens seeking a quiet place to chat.

We aimed to have as few rules as possible for the space. The guiding rule became, "You can't behave in a way that makes someone else not want to be here." Everyone didn't have to like each other, but there could be no bullying or subtle behaviors directed at excluding people.

Many inquiring families and visitors have found this commitment to hosting a space where teens could "come and go" and "sit and do nothing" questionable. Joshua and

I felt that offering the space for teens to use as they wish was an essential component of creating the non-judgmental program and relationships we envisioned, and our current staff continues to hold this view today.

Connections to the community for jobs, internships, and volunteer work

As much as we wanted to host a friendly, lively, and interesting center, we also wanted to encourage our members to spend time out in the world. As long as they weren't going to school, why should they spend all of their time with us? We didn't want our center to become an unexamined substitute for school, where kids just went during the day because they felt obligated to go somewhere.

We wanted to connect our teens with local agencies, such as the Survival Center, the Food Bank, and the Parents' Center. We suggested that they volunteer on local political or environmental campaigns. We recommended other classes, sports, and youth programs in the area. We saw ourselves as people in the center of a web, and felt it was our job to push students out to the far reaches of the network, rather than hold them all in the center with us.

This aspect of our work stretched us to build connections with all sorts of people in the community, and to discover ways our teens might learn from people and places not traditionally part of a schooling curriculum. Again, this sort of networking appealed to both Joshua and me, and we spent a good portion of our time building our literal Rolodexes (it was 1996!) and notebooks of people willing to work with our members.

Support for hobbies

Sometimes, our members figured out their paths without much direct involvement with the classes or tutoring inside our building. That first year, Jacob Abernethy worked on his juggling and magic tricks with great ambition. In school, these interests got him in trouble with teachers who were annoyed at his practicing his moves when he was bored in class.

With us, he'd come into the center and say, "Hey guys, want to see my new trick?" One day, he arrived at Pathfinder by unicycle, which caused quite a commotion. Soon he was juggling and doing tricks while perched on the unicycle in our parking lot. His mother was a doctor, and she was concerned about Jacob's lack of traditional academic output. We had several meetings to discuss whether Jacob might do more inside North Star, with limited impact.

On the positive side of things, Jacob took a calculus course at the University of Massachusetts and earned the only "A" in the class. Joshua and I both developed strong relationships with Jacob, deeper than what we had experienced with most students we had taught in school. In fact, I took Jacob for his drivers' license test and fortunately buckled my seatbelt in the back seat, so he didn't get disqualified before he shifted the car into drive.

At the end of the year, Jacob moved to eastern Massachusetts. Instead of enrolling in high school, he signed up for calculus and Latin courses at the Harvard University Community Extension program. He got a job at the Acton Science Discovery Museum as an Explainer, where he wore a white lab coat, held mirrors and magnets, and conducted physics tricks for children.

Meanwhile, he also applied for and won a slot to do performances at Quincy Market in Boston. Jacob was becoming a professional entertainer. We had helped him escape a boring high school career, to become a magician and a clown! We were on to something.

The story got even better: Jacob returned to our area to attend the University of Massachusetts Commonwealth College Honors Program in mathematics.

While there, he won the "Funniest Man on Campus" contest, and the prize was the opportunity to be the opening act for comedians Sinbad and Dave Chapelle.

Jacob then transferred as a junior to the Massachusetts Institute of Technology (M.I.T.), and has gone on to a career as a Professor of Computer Science at the University of Michigan, and—as of 2018—at Georgia Tech University.

Summary

In that first year, we wrote a handout for our recommendations for an "Independent Learning Program." We wanted to convey the idea to new families that we believed in structure, as long it was self-generated structure. The recommendations included:

1) A set of independent academic projects

2) At least one tutorial with a North Star staff member

3) Committed participation in three to six classes at North Star

4) Four to twenty hours each week of internships, volunteer work, or paid jobs

5) A weekly update meeting with a North Star staff member

6) Two to four days at North Star each week

7) Attendance at North Star community meetings

8) Attendance at some of the community events highlighted in our calendar

We did not use this set of recommendations as a checklist for pushing each member to do a little of everything. Rather, the list provided a good place to start a conversation with teens and parents who felt stuck when facing the need to create a life and routine to replace the familiarity of school.

In creating the program, Joshua and I focused on two central questions:

1) What do teens need from us, to use self-directed learning as an alternative to school? and

2) On what terms were we willing to provide those services?

Our first answers in 1996 have remained the core of the program. We have refined and expanded some over the years, but I'm always pleased when alumni from the early years visit North Star today and remark, "It still feels the same!"

7

Pathfinder

Author's Note: In the text of this chapter, I refer to our organization as North Star, in order not to confuse the reader. However, historically, at the time period covered in this chapter, its official name was Pathfinder, which is why you will read others referring to it as such.

By the fall of 1996, Joshua and I were actually supporting school-attending kids who wanted to stop going to school. Did we really know what we were doing? Looking back on it, I believe the answer is "Yes, we knew we were doing something helpful."

We saw ourselves as offering much more than just getting kids out of school: We were encouraging them to build their own lives, as if they were young adults, already finished with school.

The first conversation we had with each teen and family may have focused on "leaving," but every day after that was focused on "starting" and "doing."

We felt this way about our own work, as well. We had left teaching school, and now it was time to get started on being good at our jobs. We didn't have many doubts or qualms about our approach, and we had faith in ourselves and in the process.

We were eager to have some of our own success stories. For me, these first cases were the initial examples of what we could expect for our future careers.

Four Fellow Travelers

Among the first North Star members were four teens who had been my students at Amherst Regional Junior High

School. Their experiences were powerful for me because I could directly witness how different what they were doing at North Star was from what they had been doing in school.

Willow Hearth

If I were limited to telling the story of just one alumna to convey why and for whom I started North Star, and what this work has meant for me, I would choose to tell the story of Willow Hearth.

Willow was a friendly and serious student, who seemed willing to go along with whatever topics and assignments were part of my class. She appreciated my efforts to make things interesting and creative. However, she often struggled with doing the work. She wrote for our newsletter in January, 2000:

> I was miserable in junior high. I was not getting my work done, even though I did homework for five or six hours each night, because I worked slowly and meticulously. Though I liked all of my teachers, many of my classmates, and some of my classes, it was clear to me that something was not right. Throughout my school years, I had only two or three friends. I was not part of any after-school clubs or programs, and I only went to one school dance. I would come home and cry every day, because I was so miserable. I did not know what to do.

Sometimes, Willow would spend hours on an assignment that I had intended to take twenty minutes, or she would misunderstand the directions for an essay, such that after all of her effort, I still couldn't give it an "A" grade. I saw her tears of frustration.

She knew I cared and felt regretful, and we were riding quite the emotional rollercoaster together. Willow would later describe our relationship of that year by complimenting me, "School made me miserable, but of all my teachers you made me the least miserable."

The change I saw in Willow, from the last day of school in June to the first day of North Star in September, was extraordinary. In school, Willow had been stressed and tired and mostly alone. She made an effort to be nice to me because she liked my class.

At North Star, she was a new person. She glowed. She smiled. She had energy. She had friends. When she entered our building, or came to my class, she didn't need to try to be nice. She was now simply the person who had been suppressed in school.

We changed together. We were no longer fulfilling our roles as "teacher and student." I imagine there may have been a moment that first day or that first week or that first month when we just looked at each other inside North Star, and thought, without saying it, "Look at us! Here we are. We're really doing it."

I don't know if that moment actually occurred, but I still feel chills and get tears in my eyes as I consider the possibility. I know Willow feels the same way.

That profound experience was on day one. I had already done something more important for one individual than I may have done in my previous six years of eighth grade teaching.

It wasn't all smooth sailing, however. Willow wrote:

When I started homeschooling, I set up my week so I would have enough hours of each subject to satisfy the superintendent. I soon found that I did not have enough self-motivation. I would go to Pathfinder and talk with my friends, draw, or read, and would not start studying. While this did wonders for my self-esteem and social life, it was not so good for family relations. Every day, I had a list of things to do, and I would usually get only half of them done. This created some tension at home. My parents decided to ease up and let me pursue the subjects that I wanted, rather than the ones the superintendent needed.

While this was going on, my art was blooming. I had
been drawing all through school, in paper margins
and on the backs of worksheets, but now I had time
and encouragement. I took my sketchbooks every-
where. I also had time to experiment with Sculpey III,
a plasti-clay that I had gotten while in school. I made
miniature people, animals, and wizards.

Willow started interning for a family friend who had
created the Arts Explorium, a space for children filled with
art supplies, books, and all manner of math and science
materials. Willow was already interested in being a librarian, and the opportunity to organize the space and help
children use it was a perfect match for her.

She also took a writing course at Greenfield Community
College. When she was ready to move on from Pathfinder,
she spent a year with AmeriCorps, working in an after-
school program. She continued on to the University of
Massachusetts, earning a degree in library science.

Willow is now a circulation librarian in Arlington,
Massachusetts, and an artist with the tagline, "Magical,
mythical, or mundane, I can crochet anything!" She is
married, and feels that she is living a fulfilling life. She is a
loyal attendee at major North Star events, and we remain
in touch.

Willow's story was an important piece of my TEDx
Talk at Amherst College in 2013, where she asked me to
express the following:

Tell them I'm really content. I really like my life
now. But school was really bad for me. Sometimes
I wonder whether I would have survived four years
of high school. I think maybe you saved my life.
Thank you.

Over the years, North Star has welcomed many teens
with depression, young people who arrived with concerns
around suicide. I believe our approach has been effective in

many of these cases, and in a handful of instances, literally saved lives. I know that Willow Hearth was my first such experience of feeling, "I made the most important difference I could have made for that person, and it worked."

Tibet Sprague, Miro Sprague, John Sprague

I was surprised to see Tibet Sprague at our first informational meeting in June, 1996. He had earned straight As in school without too much effort, and he seemed well-adjusted, popular, and generally happy with his life.

It turns out that Tibet's younger brother Miro was the one interested in the meeting, but Tibet tagged along out of curiosity. I was a teacher he had liked, after all.

Much to my delight, I soon heard from his family that while Miro was going to do sixth grade at his elementary school and planned to join us the following year, Tibet was interested in joining right then.

What a great stroke of luck for us. The sad part of the story for me is that even Tibet didn't like school. A few years later, Tibet wrote in *Liberated Learners:*

> On the whole I enjoyed school. I didn't know there was any other way. Of course, I never really wanted to go to school. I hated getting up in the morning at six and dragging myself to the bus stop.
>
> In eighth grade, I couldn't stand the social system of cliques and "in" groups. I accepted that it was just the way school was...
>
> As the (first North Star) meeting went on, I discovered that deep inside I really didn't want to start ninth grade. Perhaps I had always known this, but had never been willing to admit it to myself because I thought there was no other choice. Then and there, I decided to homeschool.

One of our first converts! Here was a perfectly well-adjusted young fellow, who, given a choice, seized the chance to live a more open life than school offered. For the next four years, Tibet was a strong participant at North Star. His reflections continued:

In the second year of my self-directed education, things really took off. I started to get into the unschooling spirit by following the educational paths that were interesting and important to me. I was in a weekly writing group, I taught one of my friends to program in Java, and we spent hours together creating games. I was going to Pathfinder almost every day. My programming work with my mentor also took off. I learned five programming languages and worked for my mentor as an apprentice. I developed my own application that I displayed with him at a Boston conference. My life was wonderfully laid back, yet full of energy and learning.

I remember Tibet sitting in the Common Room near my desk many days, doing the *Boston Globe* crossword puzzle. When he was stuck, he'd shout out the clues, and sometimes I shouted back the answer. Overall, I saw Tibet put the same energy he would have put into getting good grades at school into his own priorities, and I saw the immense difference in his life.

Tibet didn't "need" North Star in any kind of urgent way, but he felt the effects of self-directed learning every bit as much as any other "struggling" teen we helped leave school.

Tibet inspired me by demonstrating just how far creative and supported teens can go during their teen years. He challenged me to reconsider my own "straight-A" high school career, and led me to wonder what I might have done with such an open opportunity.

Tibet moved on to Brown University, and has been a computer programmer and entrepreneur for the past fifteen years. He is now part of a team envisioning and consulting for positive social change.

The Sprague story doesn't stop with Tibet. His brother Miro did join us for seventh grade, and he remained a member for six years. Miro was a creative boy who always felt constrained in school, and his father told us of Miro's last day of sixth grade:

> *When Miro got off the school bus for the last time, I watched from the door as he waited until the bus was out of sight and earshot. Then he threw his book bag in the air, and hooted, hollered, and ran around the yard like a madman, jumping in the air, throwing himself to the ground, rolling around, screaming with delight. He was free at last!*

During those first years at North Star, Miro discovered his love for jazz piano. He started playing and composing jazz in his second year of homeschooling, and was soon winning national awards from *Downbeat Magazine*. He went on to the Manhattan School of Music, and then graduate school at The Thelonius Monk Institute at UCLA. He is now a world-class jazz pianist.

Following Miro's progress has certainly been a highlight of my North Star career, as he shows what happens when the mix of time, talent, practice, determination, and support is just right.

Miro and Tibet's father, John Sprague, is a Core Staff Member at North Star, and he has been part of the program just about every year from the beginning as a parent, volunteer, Board Member, and Staff Member. He holds nearly as much institutional memory as I do, and I value our almost quarter-century of working together. John celebrates how "...my children did not have to wait until age 18 to start their lives. I never knew that was possible."

For me, this quarter-century relationship with the Sprague family, including Tibet and Miro's mother Morning Star Chenven, is something I cherish, and have enjoyed with some other North Star families as well. Our model allows for the development of life-long relationships different from when I was teaching in school.

Lesley Arak

I knew Lesley before she entered my eighth grade classroom, because my wife had been her younger brother's fourth grade teacher the previous year, and we had been invited to her family's home for dinner. I thought it would be terrific to have this preliminary acquaintance as we started the year. Sure enough, Lesley and I connected around the class content.

Lesley was the sort of student who listened attentively with full eye contact, and made the appropriate faces that showed she was engaging with the material we were covering. She was a great student in person. Lo and behold, though, Lesley did not believe in completing homework.

Before long, I was on the phone with her parents, reporting her missing assignments and issuing warnings about the awful grades I would have to give her despite our lovely relationship.

I felt conflicted during these calls, but I mostly saw it as part of the job. I had some nagging guilt that I knew Lesley was learning whether or not she completed the homework assignments. In fact, she was likely thinking about the historical events we covered as much as any student I ever taught.

As that year carried on, I saw Lesley become more cynical and jaded, and I feared that both my teaching critical U.S. history and my harassments about grades only added to this process. I wasn't really having the impact I was hoping for with her.

When Lesley's parents agreed that she should leave school at the end of the year and join the inaugural year of North Star, I was ecstatic. Lesley was a perfect example of a student for whom we were creating North Star, and I was thrilled she was joining us.

Fortunately (now I'd argue, "predictably"), things worked out well on all fronts. Here's what Lesley wrote in her *Liberated Learners* essay about her two years at North Star:

During my two years of homeschooling, I also attended North Star's weekly social issues group, studied U.S. history, worked on math from time to time, and volunteered on the EcoBus, an interactive science program for the local elementary schools. I helped coach my brother's Odyssey of the Mind team, and sang in the Valley Light Opera's production of The Vagabond King. I took lots of pictures, as photography is my hobby. Over the summer of 1997, I spent three weeks in California, working as an au pair.

Perhaps even more important than all these activities, I developed better relationships with adults. I became open to their suggestions. My supervisors for the EcoBus gave me adult responsibilities with the younger students. Since I left school, adults seem to be more willing to talk to me on their own level, instead of talking down to me.

My mental state has vastly improved in my two years away from school. I feel better about myself, and I get along better with my parents.

There are many lessons to take from this short excerpt. Lesley could have been a person straight out of *The Teenage Liberation Handbook*.

For me, the primary lesson was "Yes, we are doing the right thing. Working with Lesley outside of school is better for me, better for her, and better for the world." She remains in my mind a prototypical example of teens who need our approach.

Lesley moved on to Greenfield Community College for what would have been her final two years of high school, and her photography hobby evolved into a vocation. She completed a one-year program at The Hallmark Institute of Photography, and launched her own business, Lesley Arak Photography. She remains self-employed today, and you can find her on Facebook.

Ramon Elani

In school, Ramon would come reliably to my first period class at 7:45 a.m. and quickly fall asleep. He meant no harm, and he did no harm. When he was awake, he enjoyed the primary sources and critical perspective I had to offer. He would scribble out homework, roll his eyes completing tests, and earn high grades while remaining emotionally disengaged with his school day. He came, he did, he left. Pleasantly, I reiterate.

When we started North Star, Ramon was another of my students who I hoped might join this project. School was really a waste of his time, and he was looking at four more years of navigating that course.

Ramon's parents were academics, and they had aspirations for their son. They were not going to "give up on him," but they could see the unpleasantness looming ahead in traditional high school. I was a credible enough teacher that they were at least willing to consider the idea of what we were offering.

Ramon joined, and for the next several years, he hung out at North Star doing what he might have done in school.

He enjoyed a few classes, particularly those of Joanna Weinberg Lawless, who taught Literature and Shakespeare. Ramon came to my classes, and some of Joshua's science and math classes.

Mostly, though, Ramon socialized and made wry, observant comments about the comings and goings of the people in our community.

I don't remember there being a particular moment or spark when this changed. Ramon was who he was: witty, curious, thoughtful, and above all, disengaged and cynical, in a very friendly manner. He would smile, nod, and laugh with anyone. He was part of our community, and I was fairly sure that this experience was better than anything he would have encountered in high school.

Eventually, Ramon started taking college classes in literature and philosophy, and one day I heard that he was graduating from the University of Massachusetts and going on to graduate school.

Ramon earned his Ph.D. in English at the University of Connecticut, and has taught at Hampshire College. He has had a number of other interesting experiences as an adult, including competing as an MMA fighter, and spending some time living off the grid on an island off the coast of Washington state.

He is now married and caring for his young children as his primary activity. Recently, Ramon served a term on the North Star Board of Directors. He told me he wanted to be on the Board because, "Really, North Star is the one thing in my life I'm not cynical about."

What's the lesson here? Ramon could have bumbled along through high school like a normal student. He might have eventually ended up more or less in the same place. But at age 14, he had the experience of being told, "You are right to be skeptical of the value of school. We challenge you to rise out and take yourself seriously."

Ramon took us up on that offer as best he could at that time, and the action of leaving school and being trusted to make his own decisions did leave a lasting mark on his life.

In review, the first lesson I internalized from Willow, Tibet, Lesley, and Ramon was the following: Coaching teens to leave school was likely to work well, and, even in the worst case scenario, we were very unlikely to harm anyone. We were not actually going to make anyone's life worse.

That's not how I felt when I was teaching these young people in school, and their role in demonstrating the value of the North Star approach gave me the confidence I needed to sustain this work.

In retrospect, I also see now the power of Joshua's and my role-modeling for these four teens and the others who left school with us that first year.

We weren't just pushing some theory or selling some idea. We were walking the walk. We were doing precisely the same thing we were proposing that they do: We were walking out on the security of our school jobs, in the same way they were abandoning the security of conventional school careers.

This North Star project seemed like a good idea. It sounded like a better way to live. We didn't really know for sure what would happen. We found out together.

Two Teaching Stories

Voluntary Attendance at Classes

In the first week of North Star, my expectations were shifted permanently. I was eager to begin my new life, teaching U.S. history outside of a school classroom by starting with the documentary series, *Eyes on the Prize*.

I find these videos compelling, and I obtained the *Eyes on the Prize Reader* to provide various primary documents and accounts to go along with the videos. I was ready to offer the best of the best to these lucky teens.

When that first class time arrived, I announced, "*Eyes on the Prize* starting in the classroom!" A bunch of teens stood up, but when we settled into the room, there were only three people with me. Where were the rest of them?

It turns out that they had gone outside to continue their daylong battle of fighting with foam swords, known as "boffing."

What??? These knuckleheads were skipping this amazing opportunity to watch *Eyes on the Prize* with me, so that they could play even more of their game? I proceeded with the three interested students, but I felt challenged, even angry.

"These kids don't know what's good for them," I muttered to Joshua. Here was my first lesson, in no short order. Freedom and respect for teens would have to include my acceptance that many teens did not hold my interests, or did not find my timing suitable, or had other priorities for themselves.

It was a trade-off. Would I rather have three teens who clearly want to be present, or fifteen students, including a dozen who would rather be outside clobbering each other with foam swords?

I also had to ask, "What are these teens getting out of their boffing?" Was it the chance to play, instead of attending a class? Was it making friends, in a way that some of them had never done before? Was it the joy of competing and winning? (Boffing had elaborate rules and ranks.)

In the end, does it matter? Many times in my adult life, people want me to attend a documentary or other interesting cultural event, and I feel free to decline without giving a full, detailed explanation. "No, thank you," is sufficient for me to say in these moments, and I learned to allow it to be sufficient for North Star teens.

Trail Maintenance

In the first year, I had the idea that maybe we could combine hiking and community service by offering to do some trail maintenance for the Town of Amherst's park system. I wasn't sure whom to call or if the town employees would be open to such an offer.

At that time, I carried the fear that the Town of Amherst people might not look kindly on a program that might be seen as critical of the well-regarded Amherst Regional Public Schools.

That fear was certainly misplaced. The Conservation Director welcomed my phone call, and he immediately arranged for me to meet the Conservation Department's Maintenance Worker, Nick Anzuoni.

Nick was responsible for miles and miles of hiking trails on town-owned land, and he was pretty much on his own with very little staff. He had tons of projects for us, such as brush clearing, bridge repair, sign painting, and trail marking. For a few years, I went out weekly with Nick and a group of teens and discovered many beautiful parts of Amherst. It was hard work, too.

Many different teens participated, but I particularly remember Jacob Miller-Mack's cheerfulness in carrying boards, tools, and other equipment on long, steep walks to our projects.

Nick enjoyed our company, and was happy to share his knowledge and skills with interested teens. Sometimes, I even took his lessons home with me. One day, probably when I remarked about our long, challenging hike, Nick asked, "Have you ever heard of Shackleton?"

I had not, and Nick proceeded to regale us with the story of the explorer's trip to the South Pole, where his ship was trapped in ice, and he made a heroic open water journey to save all of his men.

I went home to confirm this story, and discovered there were books, movies, and a full "Shackleton revival" going on in our culture. The Shackleton adventure became a central game in my family's home life, as my wife re-enacted parts of the story with our two young children.

This community service was glorious in its own right. North Star teens provided genuinely important and needed effort to improve our local community. We all enjoyed our days out with Nick, who was also a wildfire fighter at that time. He was patient, tolerant, and perhaps even inspired by the teens I brought along each week. The whole process was a "win-win" for everyone.

It also taught me that people would be open to our calls and our proposals. If we offered teens to do helpful work, the people and the organizations we contacted were not concerned that we were a homeschooling outfit instead of being a school. They were overjoyed at having lively, interesting young people come to their projects.

I really did not need to carry a chip on my shoulder that somehow everyone was going to be against us because we were helping teens have an alternative to school.

I also felt the strangeness of being out in public with teens during school hours. We would leave North Star in the morning, stop for errands in town, and be out in the woods, while most teens were in second or third period in school. That first year, I still knew the school schedule down to the minute, and I couldn't stop marveling at the feeling that we were out hiking in the sunshine instead of being confined to our classrooms.

Were we "getting away" with something? Was it "fair" that these teens were out here clipping bushes, instead of doing math problems? Would we be noticed or challenged by anyone? This sort of activity, and many more like it, were part of my own process of relaxing into this new world.

I didn't need to worry so much about what others thought of us. My work was to provide interesting opportunities for teens to do things with quality adults. Mission accomplished with the Amherst Conservation Department and Nick Anzuoni, and I'm pleased to report that this was the first of many such experiences for me.

Learning More Lessons

During those first years, we also learned more about the homeschooling process. One remarkable experience for me was lifelong homeschooler Kara Lewantowicz's use of our program.

At age 15, she joined North Star as a way to meet more teens and explore a community and classes in a way that was different from her previous homeschooling. She wanted to have this experience prior to jumping into full-time community college, which she did at age 17, then moved on to UMass at age 18. By age 19, she had transferred to Colorado State University as a junior, to major in Wildlife Biology.

Kara had never gone to school. She used North Star, community college, and the University of Massachusetts to end up a year ahead of teens on the traditional high school-to-college path, saving two years of out-of-state tuition at a leading program in her field.

Really? It was this simple? A healthy teen who doesn't go to school can end up ahead of her peers, while having a varied and in-depth homeschooling experience along the way? I saw the answer was "YES," in clearer terms than ever before.

Full disclosure: Kara reports that due to some credit issues within her major of Wildlife Biology, and also due to being hit by a car that led her to come home to recover for a semester, she ended up graduating from college the same year as her high-school age peers. Kara also adds, having read over this passage:

> *I would like to mention that as a child who was homeschooled for her entire life, my study skills were amazing. Now, I over-studied all of the time and part of that was because I was a sponge and enjoyed learning. Another part of that was because I was an over-achiever in everything that I did, but a big part was because I taught myself how to learn while I was a homeschooler. It was easy for me to complete homework and study for exams. My transition to college wasn't even a transition, in terms of academic skills.*
>
> *I was also very used to doing things on my own, so for me to move away to a college in Colorado and do normal life items was easy, too (e.g. grocery shopping, scheduling doctor's appointments, learning a new town, discussing incorrect charges on my student bill, etc.) I learned extreme independence and competence during my homeschool years, which I applied to my life once I left home. I have carried those skills into my adult life and into my professional life.*
>
> *I have always excelled and moved up in whatever company I have worked at. I have been told I am too efficient, too organized, and care too much about doing a good job. When I was homeschooled, I used to fear that I wasn't learning enough or learning what I was supposed to (since I had no way of knowing or quantifying where I should be). I truly believe the skills I learned as a homeschooler are still with me today! They have really made me who I am!*

Kara was just one of many North Star members who helped me appreciate the community college system and the opportunities it presents. She was an academically successful homeschooler who used community college as a first step to secondary education.

I also saw high-achieving school students, who felt bored or limited in school, use North Star as a short-term transition program and then register for full-time community college as a way to get a head start on the next phase of their lives. Ironically, one of them has gone on to a career as a public school teacher, principal, and superintendent.

Initially, I felt dismay at seeing these high-functioning teens leave North Star when they might have been juniors or seniors in high school, but once I appreciated the situation, I learned to celebrate the sight of these young people waving goodbye to North Star at young ages.

The use of community college also extended to many other teens who had not been doing well in school. One dramatic story of this era is that of Marcella Jayne. When she was a member of North Star, Marcella began her essay in our March, 2000 newsletter:

> *In school I was a freak, a punk, an outcast, and nobody at all. I was afraid to be myself and afraid to try to be anyone else. School was never an enjoyable experience for me. I was picked on for not dressing like everyone else. I was called fat, ugly, stupid, and that is how I felt.*
>
> *I tried to do well. I always did my homework and tried to keep up with my schoolwork, but from the beginning, I felt disconnected from everyone else. I felt as if I had some secret handicap that prevented me from doing as well as the others. I remember the day in the third grade when the teacher told me I was going to the Title One room during writing. I cried and screamed, "I'm not dumb!" I decided it would be my mission to prove them wrong, and I did.*

(Spoiler: Marcella accomplished her third-grade mission, many times over. She is now a corporate lawyer for Foley and Lardner LLP, in Mahattan, having graduated from Fordham University School of Law in 2018.)

Back to those teen years: Marcella did not have a lot of family support in those days, but she was good at identifying adults at North Star who could help her. She explored some interests in paganism, feminism, politics, and economics with our staff.

I remember one day driving Marcella and some classmates interested in sweatshop labor to our local mall, where they intended to identify the countries where the clothes for sale were manufactured. Apparently, they were annoying enough to the workers that they were asked to leave the premises, and I eventually returned to find them hiding in a bathroom.

Marcella had many positive experiences at North Star, but the staff worried that despite our best efforts, we might not be sufficient to help Marcella find traction to her next phase of life. In fact, when she moved on from North Star, things were pretty tenuous.

I was relieved and happy when I learned later that Marcella was at Greenfield Community College, and then that she had moved on to Mt. Holyoke College for her B.A. When she got accepted as a Stein Scholar at Fordham University School of Law, I cheered on her impressive determination.

Marcella also became the mother of two girls during these years, and expressed her intention of offering her daughters the support and stability she had craved in her childhood. Marcella's fierceness to achieve her goals educationally, professionally, and personally makes her unique among all the people I have known in my life, let alone through North Star. In fact, I suggest that Marcella's story really merits its own separate book.

In the years of 1999-2002, Marcella's path wasn't clear when she was a teenager at North Star, but her experience—layered with the others I have described in this chapter—fueled my growing conviction in our approach.

The combination of North Star's fresh start and community college's flexibility was providing a solid complementary framework for a wide range of teens wanting an alternative to high school.

Aside from these student stories, we also learned some lessons about staffing. We discovered that many people were willing to volunteer some time at North Star, as we could offer them a fairly open way of sharing what they loved with teens. They also supported our vision of providing an alternative to school for any interested teen.

The first notable volunteer we had was Joanna Weinberg Lawless, whom I met when I gave a presentation about North Star at Hampshire College, where she was a student. Joanna loved the work, and became a regular presence in the center. She taught sophisticated classes and developed several meaningful relationships with students, some of which continue to this day.

Joanna remained a Staff Member for several years, becoming the Assistant Director in 2004. As the first of many dedicated volunteers, she showed us that we might find serious, sustained contributions from skilled adults that I had not been counting on.

During these years, we also received a visit from Susannah Sheffer, the editor of *Growing Without Schooling,* the magazine John Holt had founded in 1977. She had also authored several books on homeschooling.

Joshua knew Susannah, and invited her to see what we were doing to expand the viability of unschooling to a wider community of teens and families.

Susannah arrived with some skepticism about whether we would truly be in the spirit of unschooling. We satisfied her criteria, such as her seeing that we really weren't forcing kids to do math, and that teens really were free to come and go at will.

Fortunately for us, Susannah soon moved to our area, and she began teaching a writing workshop for our members. Her work expanded to the point that Susannah became a paid member of the staff, and she remains an important Core Staff member today.

Joanna and Susannah were the first of many friends and supporters who have made North Star an interesting community. In those early years, they were among the first to commit extended time and energy to our vision. Their support was more than helpful; it was evidence that others could really see the larger goal of North Star, and would want to join in the hard work of making it a reality.

The first era of North Star, when we were called Pathfinder Center and were located in downtown Amherst, was filled with a constant set of powerful learning moments for me.

Overall, I saw how the adult world welcomed teens who felt ready to pursue their interests, with no objections to the fact that these youth had chosen to bypass traditional high school.

The End of the Beginning

By the end of this "Pathfinder Era" (2002), we knew we were on the right track. We saw our members transition from their various school identities into happy, confident young adults.

We enjoyed hosting a happy and stimulating center, and welcomed the involvement of many interested volunteers and friends. We had good relations with the community and other organizations. We were proving that there was another way to grow up, outside of school.

We saw our alumni moving on to young adulthood successfully. Tibet Sprague was at Brown University, Steve Theberge was at Columbia University, and Jacob Abernethy had transferred into the Massachusetts Institute of Technology. Our alumni were at all of our local Five Colleges: Amherst College, Hampshire College, Mt. Holyoke College, Smith College, and the University of Massachusetts, including some in the UMass Honors Program. These were North Star teens, young people whom we had coached and supported to leave school and use this approach.

The homeschooling literature was full of such stories, but now we had our own firsthand experiences.

Outside of college, Raf Anzovin had started a computer animation business with his father, and was doing work for well-known movies and studios. Jai Fuller had spent a year with the Boston Dance Company, fulfilling her goal of being a professional ballet dancer. Jacob Miller-Mack had delayed college and was working with a homebuilder. Many others had moved on to college or jobs without incident.

In fact, we began seeing that none of our alumni were actually worse off for their choice to bypass high school and start their lives earlier than expected.

Many still had difficulties; our approach wasn't a magic solution for every problem. Some teens still lacked direction, or suffered from depression, or struggled with anxiety. Nevertheless, we could see that the choice to leave school was not the limiting factor in their lives.

We began using the phrase, "We are harming no one. We are helping many people improve their lives, and making no one's life worse."

I had many conversations with my father-in-law, a cardiologist, about North Star, and he could see that I felt I was honoring the Hippocratic Oath: "First, do no harm."

This conclusion felt as important to us as our success stories. In school, we had felt that our daily work was doing some harm; now we no longer carried that burden.

Nevertheless, we faced some difficult issues. We were still in the basement of an office building, a space that had previously been a garage. It was low-ceilinged and musty. It was a good place for the excitement of a start-up operation, but it didn't feel professional.

A larger problem, however, was that Joshua and I were still earning small salaries. We held a commitment to having a relatively low membership fee and to welcoming all interested teens, regardless of their families' ability to pay that fee. The revenue was not growing as we needed.

We decided it was time to find a more professional space, incorporate our own non-profit, and work on fund-raising to address these issues.

In 2002, we became North Star: Self-Directed Learning for Teens, and moved to the neighboring town of Hadley in a well-lit, professional-looking office space in a building also occupied by Sylvan Learning Center. We were on to the next phase.

8

Onward

Sometimes, I imagine North Star as a year-long cruise ship adventure. For the first several years, we were a merry band on a rickety houseboat, welcoming newcomers at all ports. Those on board seemed to fare well, but a cursory look at the enterprise was sure to generate some hesitation and skepticism. In 2002, we traded up for a more secure vessel, and soon brought on some new crew. We tidied things up, expanded some of our activities, and formalized the process for families joining the adventure.

As we outgrew this second home, then-Program Director Catherine Gobron set her sights on an old, vacant, and impressive-looking ship dry-docked just down the way. In a bold maneuver, Catherine approached the owners and soon we were floating along in digs beyond anything I had imagined was possible. It was eight years before the authorities finally declared the boat unworthy and forced us to abandon ship. With a stroke of luck, we found a similar-sized but more modern ship one harbor over, which we occupy today.

I don't know why this metaphor amuses me, but somehow I enjoy the idea that North Star is an adventure boat welcoming teens at various ports, who travel along with us for as long as they wish.

Out on the sea, we do as we please, and our crew and passengers pursue a different set of goals than people pursue on conventional trips. Each yearly adventure has a slightly different cast of characters and somewhat different memories. We voyage in familiar waters, but I enjoy sharing the sights and possibilities with each new traveler. It's what we are doing, the way we are doing it, and with whom we are doing it that keeps me fresh and intrigued. I suppose that being out in the metaphorical fresh air every day helps, too.

As I review the past fifteen years, I find it hard to identify specific highlights without feeling that I'm leaving out important people. Just as I did in the previous chapter, I would like to mention some of the people and stories that have shaped my view of what we are accomplishing at North Star.

Staffing

The dominant character of the Hadley era (2002-2015) was Program Director Catherine Gobron. Catherine joined the North Star staff in a minor role in 2003, just as co-founder Joshua Hornick and longtime volunteer and then-Assistant Director Joanna Weinberg Lawless were moving on.

At that time, Catherine was homeschooling her two children, ages six and two, and appreciated the flexibility of a part-time position at North Star. Further, Catherine had hated high school, and felt eager to offer an alternative to teens she related to, due to her personal experience.

As Catherine's role grew from part-time to full-time, she implemented her vision for North Star, which included a more robust academic program. She wanted to improve and professionalize North Star's operation, and its image in the community.

For the most part, I had been focused on offering an alternative-to-school for teens feeling bored or constrained. Catherine wanted to create quality programs in their own right—such as writing, theatre, travel, and other academic areas—such that North Star would become the first choice for many families, rather than a place-of-last-resort for desperate families. Her ambition and initiative fueled this phase of North Star.

She recruited volunteers and work-study students from local colleges to fill out the program. She started

a weekly blog. She organized and led annual commu-
nity service trips to New Orleans, and then to various
Spanish-speaking destinations, including Vieques, Puerto
Rico and Nicaragua.

Catherine initiated and led North Star's move to the
Russell Street School building in Hadley, in 2007. The first
time I saw our giant black sign hanging out front by Route
9, it gave me chills I will always remember. We had truly
arrived, it seemed to me.

Catherine found a willing staff and parent community
to join in these efforts, and collectively, North Star grew
during this era. We nearly doubled in size, from an annual
membership averaging 30-40 members to one averaging
60-75 members. Our budget tripled. Our public image
and our relationships with other community organizations
became more professional.

Perhaps predictably, Catherine dreamed of starting
her own program from scratch, in a community she felt
dearly needed it: Holyoke, Massachusetts. For a variety of
reasons, Catherine felt connected to this largely Spanish-
speaking community, with dismal public schools that had
been seized by the State Board of Education, due to their
poor outcomes. Catherine wanted to establish a North Star-
type alternative program for the Puerto Rican young people
in that community.

In 2015, as North Star was moving to its new home in
Sunderland, Massachusetts, Catherine announced that she
and former North Star Board Member Josiah Litant were
establishing Lighthouse Holyoke.

Spring, 2015, was the end of both the Hadley era
and the Catherine era for North Star, and we celebrated
Catherine's important contributions to North Star at our
fundraising brunch that May. (There is more on the similarities and differences between Lighthouse Holyoke and
North Star in Chapter 11.)

Fortunately, Loran Saito was a board Member at this
time, and she was ready for more direct involvement with
the day-to-day running of the program. Her four children

were current members or alumni of North Star. Loran shared Catherine's commitment to quality and attention to detail, and as our current Program Director, she has continued North Star's program in her own professional manner.

The Core Staff

One step in professionalizing our work was establishing a system to check in with each of our members on a weekly basis. The Staff Members who conducted these advisory meetings became the Core Staff, and as a group, this team has maintained the vision and responded to issues together. The team has remained stable for many years, and I deeply value our working relationships.

As of 2018, in addition to Loran Saito and myself, the long-term Core Staff includes:

- Ellen Morbyrne, an alumna from our early Pathfinder years (1996-2001), who returned to direct our Theatre Program around 2004. She has remained a key presence, even as she went through Smith College, got married, and now has two children of her own (who are homeschooling, of course!).
- Susannah Sheffer, our direct connection to John Holt, has been part of North Star for nearly two decades. Her experience with and vision for unschooling provide a depth of knowledge for our community. Her psychology- and justice-related classes are some of North Star's more sophisticated offerings.
- John Sprague, already mentioned in Chapter 4, has been an integral part of North Star's history.
- Joshua Wachtel, who volunteered with North Star in 2010, joined our staff when we needed another advisor. His skill set, intuition, and positive outlook have contributed to our community. Joshua, with John's support, is largely responsible for the development of our music program and the North Star Band.
- Jodi Lyn Cutler, whose son was a member of North Star 2007-2010, served on our Board of Directors from 2009-2015. Her energy, vision, and success in that

role made her the first choice when we needed a new Outreach Director in 2015. Her creativity and focus have been integral to North Star's growth.

- Melanie Dana, who had been homeschooling her two children prior to their joining North Star, began volunteering at North Star in 2013. She taught math and science classes, and was generous with her time and concern. When we had our most recent surge in membership in 2016, Melanie was the obvious choice to join the Core Staff.

Other Staff

When Joshua Hornick was leaving the North Star staff in 2003, he helped initiate our relationships with local colleges and universities, allowing us to become an off-campus work-study venue. This means that college students receiving work-study allotments as part of a financial aid package can work at North Star. North Star is responsible for an "agency portion" of their wage, which ranges from 10%-20% of the hourly wage. This arrangement has been a terrific source of tutors and mentors from our local college community.

We also have welcomed college students earning community service credits or independent study coursework credit for their involvement at North Star. Also, as previously mentioned, numerous adult volunteers have contributed to our program. The overall growth of North Star's capacity is the result of thoughtful attention to all of these staffing opportunities.

Board of Directors

This era of North Star also saw a major shift in the work of our Board of Directors. In 2012, Gary Bernhard became President of the Board, and he has successfully nurtured a culture of action and fundraising by this group. Gary has a long history in alternative education, including a long-term position as the Director of the University Without Walls at the University of Massachusetts. He possesses a full career worth of experience in building alternative paths for people of all ages, who feel trapped in traditional education.

In the past decade, the Board has developed an annual routine of events aimed at raising the funds necessary to cover North Star's fee reductions. These events demand energetic participation and leadership from the Board. The monthly meetings, along with various additional committee meetings, have become a priority for all Board members.

Gary promotes his strong vision for improving and stabilizing North Star's financial position. His leadership has inspired a range of people to serve on the Board, and their good work has played an important role in North Star's growth. I appreciate them all, though I am recognizing only Gary here, due to my concern about starting an incomplete list.

More Teen Stories

Over the past fifteen years, there have been many teens whose actions have helped shape my understanding of our work. Here are some of my highlights:

Jen Eckard

One frequently asked question is whether we ever receive push-back from schools about encouraging teens to leave school to pursue self-directed learning. The answer is, "Rarely, to the point of 'No.'"

The one exception was the case of Jen Eckard, in which one of her high school teachers called me at home, absolutely indignant that I was supporting Jen to walk out on "...a stellar, AP high school career, bound for a good college."

I tried to explain that North Star could be a different means to the same end, but this teacher was unconvinced and hung up angry.

Jen was a member of North Star for just one year. Five years later, she joined me on a panel presentation for Compass Centre in Ottawa, Quebec. In her speech, Jen stated:

I was a "straight-A" student. I was very successful in school. Nobody ever would have expected that I was going to leave school.

I was doing what I was supposed to do: I was jumping through all the hoops, I was getting the As. I knew I was going to go to college and get some kind of safe job, and everything was going to be cool. I just kind of assumed that was what I needed to do.

I was not enthusiastic about it. I was very bored with it. I wasn't doing what I cared about. I wasn't satisfied with my life. I wanted something different.

Then I found out about North Star, and that I didn't have to be there (in school). I just went there for a year. I was 16. I soaked up everything I could from North Star in a year, and then I felt it was time for me to move on.

The main thing that happened was—and I had no idea at the time that this was going to be so important—I took a yoga class at North Star. I had this really amazing experience in the class that was really inspiring for me. A family friend told me about Kripalu, the largest yoga center in North America, and I ended up going there during the year that would have been my senior year in high school.

I spent six months living at Kripalu, learning about yoga, meditation, Eastern philosophy, and all these things that I had had no exposure to in school. It was incredibly exciting to me. I felt it was where I belonged. I ended up taking massage therapy training there, and getting my certification. I got my massage license when I was 19, and started working.

I like my life. I feel good about it, and I didn't go to university. Some people who knew me in school might be shocked at that, but I feel much better off.

I'm a much happier person. I know who I am.

I'm really grateful to North Star. I always tell people I hope I become a millionaire, so I can give a bunch of money to North Star.

The irony is that the angry teacher's fears proved true. Jen walked out on an exceptional high school career in 2003, and as of this writing, she has yet to attend college. Jen remains in touch with both Catherine and me, and is a local alumna we count on whenever we need someone to represent North Star.

Raphaela Levy-Moore

Similar to Jen, Raphaela left high school with excellent grades, feeling constrained by the system. Raphaela, however, used her freedom to seriously pursue her academics in a more thorough and satisfying way than she had felt able to do in her high school classes.

She was actively involved with North Star classes such as Literature and Shakespeare. She took classes at Greenfield Community College, Hampshire College, and Amherst College as a teen, then spent a "gap year" pursuing a series of volunteer service travel opportunities around the globe. Her self-made transcript (see Appendix I) of her years out of school remains one of the most compelling documents I have read in the homeschooling literature.

Raphaela went on to Amherst College and has been working in the business world since her graduation. Her focus and self-presentation expanded my understanding of what can happen when the energy used to obtain straight As in school is applied to pursuing one's own interests.

Ben Rosser

The staff at North Star have a standing joke, which is how long it takes a parent to utter the phrase, "...but what about math?" As in, "My child is happy, our family is happy, it's a miracle how North Star has improved our lives, and we are eternally grateful. But, what about math?"

One of our best math-related stories comes from Ben Rosser, whose experience helped give me a clear answer to other parents.

Ben came to North Star at age eleven, and stayed for six years. He was fun, charismatic, and talented. He played sports. He mastered the guitar. He was a naturalist, outdoorsman, and skier. He took a bladesmithing class and held a long-term jewelry-making apprenticeship. He eventually took up photography. He was a friend to everyone, and his family hosted our year-end parties at their home. Ben was a central figure at North Star.

But Ben did not do math. Every attempt he made to memorize his multiplication tables and use formulas ended in frustration. He could do anything with his hands, but he seemed to have no space in his brain for the abstractions of theoretical mathematics. Ben's mother, Carol Hetrick, wrote about her experience with this situation for our newsletter, in Winter 2010:

When Ben was thirteen, he still couldn't do math. As I saw it, he seemed to understand the basic concepts, but he could do very little on paper. He certainly didn't know his multiplication tables or how to do long division. He also had no interest in learning it any further. This concerned me very much. I gave in to my doubt again and we had a heart-to-heart talk. Reluctantly, he agreed to sit down every day and do math.

It wasn't long before this became problematic. Ben began resisting and I had to nag him daily to do it. This was a real drag. Finally, Ken Danford persuaded me to let it go. It took all my inner strength to indulge in this experiment.

Three years went by, and still no interest in math.

Finally, at age 16, Ben and his girlfriend decided they wanted to take an advanced photography course at Holyoke Community College. He aced the language placement exam and flunked the math test with a 20 percent (score). This being the first test he'd ever taken, he was hardly fazed by the score. He would just take the test again.

Well, it fazed me a lot. Early December arrived, and I began reminding him that time was getting short. Finally, he snapped back at me one day with great impatience, not his usual style.

"Mom! I'll pass it!"

Yikes.

Next thing I knew, he decided to go on a ski trip with his best friend over the Christmas holiday. Oh, man. The test date was January 7. There was nothing I could do.

As fate would have it, Ben's friend's father, Bill, who was taking them on the ski trip, is an MIT graduate with a strong background in math. By prior agreement, he brought a math book on the ski trip. Every day for five days, Ben and Bill did math together in the ski lodge for an hour-and-a-half, over lunch.

The following week, I drove Ben to Holyoke Community College and held my breath throughout the entire exam. I felt so uncomfortable. Ben emerged from the test, calm and cool as a cucumber. He looked me in the eye with a very sweet smile and said, "I got a hundred. I'm good at math."

I haven't been the same since.

Ben took the photography class, and he has gone on to be a professional photographer in New York City.

The lesson I took from this experience is not that Ben Rosser is a natural mathematician. I have told Ben directly that I don't plan to drive over any bridges he builds. The main lesson is that when people who are confident in many areas finally have to confront a weakness in order to proceed with their strengths, they can use their confidence to overcome feeling vulnerable in an area they have avoided.

Ben finally needed to do math, and as a capable and successful young person in other areas, he was able to focus and deal with this obstacle. The minor lesson in this story is that the math required to pass an entry-level community college placement exam is not complicated stuff.

Ben's story, and others like his, have shown us that supporting teens to identify strengths and feel confident in at least one area is an excellent strategy for helping them deal with their weaknesses in the future.

Sphennings Wright

North Star Staff Members allow teens to define their own pace for growing up. Many teens are in a hurry to become independent young adults. One memorable story is just the opposite.

Sphennings came to North Star at age 14, fairly annoyed with and resistant to all the adults who had been pestering him to shape up and do well in school. Sphennings was perfectly capable of reading and writing, but he didn't feel like doing things for the sake of others.

At North Star, he adopted this new name, Sphennings, on his first day, and seized on the chance to re-invent himself. He was a very positive and committed member of North Star, and he rode his bike an hour each way to get to us. As the years wore on, Sphennings displayed no desire to take a college course, find a part-time job, or get a drivers' license. At age 16, in our family meetings, Sphennings resisted all invitations, offers, and bribes to get on with things. He preferred the limits and inconveniences of the middle-teen years to moving on.

Once, when we pressed him to explain himself, he stood up, shrugged, reached out with his arms, and declared, "I really messed up my early teen years, when I was 12-14. At North Star, I'm re-doing those years, and

I'm quite happy with how it's going. I'm not done doing this yet. Let me finish."

Sphennings did move beyond North Star successfully, has held a number of jobs, and attended the University of Alaska-Anchorage for four years without graduating ("The last thing I graduated from was elementary school," he informed me for this book.) He now works as a software developer. I thank Sphennings for holding true to his own inner clock and including me in his journey.

David Rainville and Isaac Yglesias

Over the years, North Star has welcomed several members diagnosed with various learning differences and equipped with special education plans. When they join us, we treat these young people exactly as we treat all new members of North Star: We ask them about their strengths and weaknesses, and we allow them to define their own priorities and schedules.

We do not make them start with working on their weaknesses, which often is a refreshing relief for both the students and the parents. We tend to avoid reading various school documents that outline detailed analyses and strate-gies for these young people, unless the student and parents strongly request that we do so.

Instead, we allow the students to enter our community, explore our classes, request one-on-ones, and consider a weekly routine in the exact same manner we do with every new member.

We observe their choices and behaviors, and we ask them how they feel about their time at North Star. We are curious to know how they spend their time outside of our building, during the evenings and weekends. Do they have any clubs, sports, hobbies, or academic pursuits that they love? Would they like any support in these areas? Are there any activities that are particularly difficult, with which they would like some help?

Our philosophy incorporates Howard Gardner's sense of multiple intelligences, and we assume everyone has gifts and talents that they may want to nurture. I relish being the adult who offers this "start with your strengths" approach to teens who have dreaded going to school for years, and hear this invitation as some sort of long-dreamed-of gift.

The two young men I profile in this section, David Rainville and Isaac Yglesias, didn't need this offer from North Star—to start with their strengths—because they had been attending Four Winds School, a small middle school that is modeled after a one-room schoolhouse, with an individually determined curriculum for each student.

David's mother Ellen explains, "Four Winds is innovative in its attention to each individual, and is traditional in the quality and rigor of the education. It is the best of both worlds." Had Four Winds offered a high school program, both David and Isaac would have stayed there. Since Four Winds stopped at ninth grade, these families were seeking a similar environment for high school.

Both David and Isaac were avid readers, and they each pursued their intellectual interests independently and thoroughly. David was especially interested in history, anthropology, and philosophy. Isaac had passions for geography and economics, and he loved studying atlases and census data.

Both boys arrived at North Star open to our staff and community. They each attended a range of classes and requested several tutorials, using North Star in their own ways, just like every other member. In Isaac's case, these tutorials included some social skills, exploration of our local community, and adventures in how to take the public bus, as well as for his academic interests.

Both David and Isaac knew what they wanted to do and how they wanted to do it. They both had very supportive, trusting, and patient parents. When these fellows graduated from Four Winds, they were facing a hard moment.

Both might have attended public or private school successfully, given the support of their parents and the staff at any school. But both would have been labeled with diagnoses and given special programs. Neither would have felt comfortable in the commotion and crowd of a large school.

Isaac found social groups confusing, and he struggled to understand the social nuances of his peers in a group setting. He also would have spent a lot of time trying to interpret and conform to rules and expectations that he didn't fully understand. David did often interact with his peers, but he found the effort exhausting. He liked conversations and classes, but he found himself feeling spent after this sort of engagement.

North Star gave each of them complete control over how many days to attend, and how to spend their time when they were present. At North Star, providing this self-determination isn't so much a strategy as it is a foundational premise.

We believe David, Isaac, and all of our members have a basic right to choose how to spend their time. They get to define their own goals and set their own limits. This contrast to traditional schooling is particularly dramatic in these cases, which would have involved special education attention in schools.

David wrote in a 2012 letter to his new academic advisor at Hampshire College:

> *At North Star, I relished talking to smart, passionate people, reading in the small but eclectic library, or even finding a private space to sit and think. But the best part was having the freedom to do almost whatever I wanted, practically whenever I wanted.*
>
> *My favorite course was, without a doubt, anthropology. The teacher obviously loved his subject and knew it back-to-front. The topic itself helped me put the rest of the world in perspective, though over time I've found what I learned there to be less than holy writ. After that, I had a philosophy/world religions class that I loved because it introduced me to my beloved philosophy, and sometimes hated because the teacher couldn't always tell the difference between philosophy and world religions.*

*The hardest part of North Star was balancing a
social life with my need to be alone. There were a lot
of brilliant people there, but most of the time I agreed
with Sartre: "Hell is other people."*

*It comes down to one word: freedom. Freedom to
study what interests me, in a way that interests me.
Freedom to balance solitude and interaction as best
suits me, and to change it as I see fit.*

North Star served David and Isaac well, and they each
moved on to community college and then to four-year
colleges. David has graduated from Hampshire College,
and is now enrolled in a Masters Degree program at
Western New England School of Law, aiming to work in the
field of labor law. Isaac is now at Brandeis University, having
completed a semester abroad in Cuba, in 2017.

There is something rather simple in these stories. We
asked David and Isaac what they wanted to learn, and we
met with their parents on a regular basis. We did the best
we could to creatively help them accomplish their goals.
These are the stories that fill me with confidence in the
power of self-directed learning. There is just no way that
I could have made the same difference in their lives if I
had been their ninth-grade history teacher in school, and I
doubt they would have moved along in school as they did
through our approach.

Alex Rosenbach

In April, 2018, I received an email from alumnus Alex Rosenbach. He had moved on from North Star
in 2015, and had been attending Holyoke Community
College. He wanted to share his news with several adults
and mentors in his life:

*I've just received news that I got accepted
as a transfer into RIT's (Rochester Institute of
Technology's) game design program, one of the
most competitive departments in the country, that*

doesn't even consider transfers most of the time. This wouldn't have been possible without all your help and encouragement!

He included a sentence or two for each adult, making it a lovely note, and his words for me were:

Ken, you helped me through the roughest and darkest time of my life. I don't know where I'd be if it weren't for you. You have an amazing program that allows kids to learn in an environment that is more personable and allows you to do what you want, based on your choices and passions!

His story is particularly unique. Alex was born deaf, and he received his first cochlear implant when he was two years old. He attended Clarke School for the Deaf when he was young, which went well for him. As he reached upper elementary school age, his parents decided to mainstream him into the local public schools.

His mother was a teacher in the system, and his father was a speech and language therapist. Unfortunately, things didn't go smoothly, and by middle school, Alex was experiencing depression and declaring he didn't want to go to school.

When he arrived at North Star, Alex was 14 years old. He had a twinkle in his eye, and seemed friendly and curious, despite his woes with school.

He seemed to be a fairly common sort of 14-year-old boy, who was disorganized in school, labeled and isolated in a special program, and forced to work on his weaknesses every day. The fact that he was deaf seemed secondary to me. North Star had no special approach to working with deaf teens, so we just went about our normal process.

At first, Alex attended North Star irregularly, and mostly wanted to spend his time socializing. He also liked sitting in our quieter spaces, as the noise of the Common Room could be physically unpleasant for him.

He developed a strong relationship with his advisor, Catherine Gobron, and in his second year, Alex had several tutorials, including writing, math, and history. In his third year, Alex participated in some of our classes and focused on getting his GED with a tutor. Still, Alex preferred playing games, both video games and board games such as chess, to studying traditional academics.

He was always cheerful and friendly at North Star, and he seemed to be maturing at his own pace. When he missed out on activities or announcements, it was hard for us to know whether it was because of his hearing issues or because he just didn't want to do them.

Alex's parents worried a lot about Alex during these years. He liked his friends and his games, and he was a kind, sweet person. But he wasn't finding any serious direction. They wondered, "What should we do?"

North Star staff consistently said, "Wait. Remain calm. Alex is a delightful person. He'll be okay."

In retrospect, his mother, Renata, says, "You gave us shelter. You offered hope to the whole family by showing us there were plenty of different visions possible."

When Alex moved on to Holyoke Community College at seventeen years old, we didn't know how things would go. It turned out that Alex thrived there. He took himself seriously, and HCC provided the accommodations he needed for his hearing issues.

I attribute Alex's positive outcomes to the power of our approach. Like many young people who are frustrated and angry in school, Alex just wanted to be left alone. He didn't want to focus on things he found boring or difficult. He had no bad intentions, so why couldn't he just be allowed to play his games and be nice to people? He'd get serious about something eventually, he figured.

Fortunately for Alex, his parents accepted our perspective, and held their concerns while they watched Alex grow up for three years at North Star. We were all in this together, and it turns out that patience and trust were what Alex needed most of all.

Independent Homeschoolers

Most North Star members come from school, and would not be homeschooling without North Star. However, each year we do have some experienced homeschoolers join us, and I have appreciated learning from them as well.

McKenzie and Sage Wilson

McKenzie and Sage moved to our area when they were approximately 14 and 12 years old, respectively. They were successful homeschoolers, but didn't know people in the Pioneer Valley. On the first day they visited North Star, one of our Staff Members had arranged a "Goth Photo Day," and many teens were scurrying about the building in rather outlandish black makeup and attire.

I was a bit worried that these 'Happy Homeschoolers' were having this introduction to our community, but amusingly enough, it was the perfect event for them.

McKenzie and Sage loved the scene they beheld, and with their parents, Ananda and Eric, they became fixtures at North Star for several years. A vibrant, existing, stable, fun community of 60 teens was just what they had dreamed of, and they set about participating in and contributing to our program. Both McKenzie and Sage welcomed having a North Star Staff Member as an advisor; an adult with whom they could imagine, discuss, and plan things in a different way than they did with their parents.

Ananda became a teacher and mentor for other teens at North Star. Our set of services and our non-coercive approach were perfect for this family at these ages.

McKenzie has since moved on to full-time college study, and Sage is now a professional ballet dancer. They are both extraordinarily fun and talented people. Their participation, and that of others like them, has helped me see North Star from a fresh perspective. They didn't need our help to get out of school and learn about a different way to live; they simply wanted an interesting and healthy community. The reality that we could be that place for them granted a different kind of confirmation for me about the quality of our program.

Aidan Urschel

Sometimes, this homeschooling process works in the reverse order. I coach teens to leave school, then they discover they don't want or need North Star, either. They can be successful, independent homeschoolers on their own. One excellent example of this path is Aidan Urschel.

Aidan came to North Star at age 12, rather angry at his cozy private school for doing everything "wrong." He just wanted to learn things his own way. His parents—college-educated, professional, and community-engaged—had no familiarity with homeschooling. They were concerned when Aidan came to North Star, tolerated us, but exhibited no real passion for our community or our staff.

Aidan is a unique person, who has strong interests in welding, carpentry, and all hands-on creative "making" enterprises. He also had a desire to protect others, first exhibited by making first-aid kits he could hand out, and later by being the youngest participant in the Amherst Community Emergency Response Team (CERT) training at age 14.

Aidan's parents identified and hired some excellent people to be tutors and mentors for Aidan, and they were superb at exposing Aidan to a variety of organizations and events in our community. After two years at North Star, Aidan's lack of enthusiasm for his time in our building was painful to witness. It took a bit of cheerleading by me to convince Aidan's parents that they were naturals for this task, and that they could homeschool without us. Aidan had better ways to spend his time, instead of humoring his parents by being present in our building.

Aidan has grown into a leader in several homeschooling groups and other activities. He is mature, and because of his CERT training, I currently count on him to protect me in a catastrophe. Aidan and his family may have needed me to explain to them that "school is optional," but beyond that, they didn't need North Star any more than they needed school. I embrace this learning. Thank you, Aidan, Sydne, and John.

The End of the Middle

North Star spent thirteen years in Hadley (2002-2015), during which time we came to see our work in fresh and deeper ways. We improved and professionalized our operations, and we worked with a range of teens and families who helped us see the strengths and possibilities for our model. It's been a team effort of staff, teens, parents, and our wider Pioneer Valley community.

The hundreds of cases have provided me with the confidence and joy I have needed to make sharing this approach my life's work. This chapter has only scratched the surface of describing some of the people who have shown me how the self-directed learning process can play out over time.

For me, the most powerful lesson is that trusting teens works. Our most important tasks are to listen and to trust. We can provide feedback, suggestions, and invitations. Sometimes we even get to directly teach things. I hope that sharing these stories may inspire others to extend their patience and their vision for self-directed learning.

In 2015, we moved to Sunderland, and the process has continued rather seamlessly. The program, the teens, and the work have continued on the same path. My work has changed somewhat, as I have expanded my efforts to consult with others wanting to replicate our model (see Chapter 11). The Sunderland Era mostly feels like a smooth continuation of the previous years in Hadley, with ongoing improvements as we continue to reflect on our best practices and outcomes.

In January, 2017, I published a study with the Alliance for Self-Directed Education about our alumni outcomes (see Appendix II). In Chapter 10, I will revisit that study and reflect on more data that supplements these anecdotes.

9

The Hard Parts

Joshua and I had spent the better part of two years, when we were teaching in public school together, complaining about various aspects of our jobs to each other. Prior to knowing Joshua, I had spent plenty of time complaining about my difficulties teaching to any friend, family member, or acquaintance who wanted to listen. Everybody we knew had attended school and could imagine our jobs, so they could relate to our predicament in some way.

This process shifted dramatically for me when we started North Star. I had very little to complain about in terms of students and my workday. I woke up looking forward to going to work, and I enjoyed most of my time at the center. I no longer had the regular sorts of teacher complaints about students and schooling.

Instead, I faced an entirely different set of problems. The three largest were: money, the public image and public understanding of North Star, and hard cases of teens and families.

Money

I have felt some stress around the North Star budget every day since we opened in September, 1996. There is a cliché that in homebuilding projects, you can only have two out of three variables: on-time, on-budget, and high quality. At North Star, those three variables would be modest membership fees, inclusion of low-income families, and professional wages for staff. It's hard to close a budget triangle that includes those three corners. However, we have not wanted to have a private school level tuition, for fear of scaring away potential member families.

We have always held a one-hundred-percent-firm commitment to welcoming all families, regardless of their ability to pay the full fee. These two non-negotiable principles have left staff salaries as the open corner of the triangle. North Star has always struggled to pay full and appropriate salaries to its staff.

Our model as a non-profit organization has been to solicit donations and conduct fundraisers to close the gap, and to a decent extent, we have been successful in recent years. But for our first ten to fifteen years, we did not achieve our goals, and money was the number one daily issue we confronted.

It's hard for me to complain about budget woes to others. I walked away from a secure job with good wages and benefits to start this program, and I knew the challenge we were facing when I did so. Further, I have the good luck to have had some family resources from my own grandmothers that have allowed me to live with the modest and insecure salaries at North Star. I could share our difficulties with others, but I couldn't complain.

Unfortunately, the lack of fully appropriate staff salaries is the main reason co-founder Joshua Hornick moved on after seven years of work here, and it's why other central Staff Members have moved on as well. Just about every other program modeled after North Star shares this budget problem, and struggles to balance the choices of membership fees, scholarships and inclusion, and staff salaries.

Currently, the North Star annual budget is approximately $375,000-$400,000. Membership fees make up about two-thirds of the revenue, with fundraising and donations comprising the remaining third. Our expenses are nearly two-thirds personnel, with the final third being rent, fixed costs, and discretionary costs.

This budget stress shows no signs of abating, and I currently believe the best solution will be putting some serious effort into creating an endowment of $2 million or more for North Star, which would guarantee a significant portion of the budget each year. Stay tuned.

In the meantime, I am able to share that managing the budget, and having North Star pay lower salaries than I wish, has been the most stressful part of this work, without question.

Public Image and Public Understanding of North Star

Earlier, I described how it has been difficult for me to succinctly explain North Star to interested newcomers. At the same time, we've had to face various assumptions and statements in our local community about our work.

Some of these have been complimentary, others rather negative. Some of the confusion is of our own making, due to our own lack of a strong branding and marketing presence. Here are some of the common misperceptions we have heard over the years:

The Positive
- North Star is mostly for gifted and unusually self-directed kids.
- North Star is for kids who want to homeschool and have good relationships with their parents.
- North Star is for highly functional parents who just need a bit of help for their kids.

The Negative
- North Star is mostly dropouts and bad kids.
- North Star lets the kids smoke pot and sit there stoned all day.
- North Star is for kids who can't cut it in any regular school.
- North Star is for lazy kids whose irresponsible parents are letting them take the easy way out.
- North Star kids just sit around and do nothing.
- North Star Staff Members ignore the kids.

A major purpose of this book is to dispel all these myths, so I'll just scratch the surface here. The main point

I want to make in this section is that dealing with North Star's public image has been a constant challenge.

In 2010, we finally created the position of Outreach Director, whose job it was to work on these issues. Since then, the efforts of our staff, board, alumni, and general community have made a lot of progress in this area.

It turns out that putting good energy into marketing matters, and having some paid staff to focus on this topic matters even more.

Our Outreach Directors have extended the scope of our newsletter, *Liberated Learners*, filling it with news, photos, and profiles of many community members. They have launched and grown our Facebook page, which in this modern world is an important platform for sharing photos and passing along good news. They have improved our website and brochures, making each connection to North Star feel more aesthetically pleasing and professional for inquiring people.

They have contributed to making our building more welcoming and homey through art, furniture, and attention to detail. They have attended Chamber of Commerce events, independent school fairs and other gatherings, to present North Star to our local business community. They have attended Board of Directors meetings, and taken the lead to implement the projects that group brainstorms to enhance North Star's stability.

In 2007, we held our first Celebration of Self-Directed Learning, during which we present an award to a local adult who has thrived, despite not completing high school. We use this moment to gather our community and host an elegant banquet, asserting our identity and confidence in our alternative path.

In 2014, North Star began a high profile public event every summer, hosting Circus Smirkus, a spectacular traveling youth circus. In these ways, along with some limited advertising, we put our best foot forward in our community.

The most successful element in improving our public image, though, has been the slow and steady work of making a difference for our members. We act professionally by doing what we claim to do: offering a positive difference in people's lives.

I believe that word-of-mouth conversations and referrals are our most powerful tools, and after more than 20 years, we now have a great many alumni, parents of alumni, volunteers, and others who have interacted with North Star. The steady flow of positive feelings and stories based on our efforts, one child at a time, has made a difference. In North Star's case, longevity matters. We have had the time for more and more people to get to know us, which has worked to our benefit.

Cigarettes and Marijuana

When we started, Joshua and I had no real plan about building our image, and no real sense of what we would be facing. I think my first bit of dismay came in that first month, when I realized that some of our newly recruited members smoked cigarettes. Neither Joshua nor I smoked, and we had no patience with the habit. We certainly weren't going to permit teens to smoke in our center, and we figured we could say no smoking on the premises, either. But where was the limit?

Schools don't stop kids from walking to town after school and smoking cigarettes, so why should we? What if kids went for a walk uptown and smoked? Was that our business? We weren't entirely sure. However, when a handful of North Star members started stepping just off of our premises to congregate and start smoking, we knew we had a problem.

We wouldn't bring our children to a program where a bunch of teens were smoking, and we found it unappealing ourselves, as well. The rule eventually became that kids could go for a walk and smoke, but that they should be out of sight of our building.

We were in a bit of a lose-lose situation, being associated with teens smoking, but we did the best we could. In fact, in our private meetings with teens and parents, we would raise the cigarette smoking behavior and ask if the teen might want any support from us to quit the habit.

We never considered prohibiting cigarette smokers from joining North Star. We lived with this poor public image problem for many years, as part of the landscape of working with all interested teens. Much to my delight, over the past several years, this problem has nearly ceased to exist. I am not aware of any current or recent members being teens who smoke cigarettes during their days at North Star.

With any luck, this trend is part of a decreasing smoking habit among teens in the United States. (Alas, as I write this section in 2018, it appears that vaping is a new, fast-growing habit among teens, one that is just occasionally appearing at North Star.)

For the most part, marijuana use by our teens at North Star has been more of an image issue than a factual problem. We have always had some members who experimented with marijuana in their teen years, and a handful who used it regularly. There have been some who have violated our policy and come to North Star while under the influence of pot.

As much as possible, we have confronted these teens, asked them to leave, and held meetings with their families to determine whether to continue their membership.

Over two decades of working with teens, there have been moments when groups of teens have violated this policy together. Unfortunately, it seems to me that a few such moments have had a lasting impact on our public image, based on the occasional comments I get from inquiring parents worried about our teen culture.

Our experience is that many teens report that there is far less marijuana use among North Star teens than at the previous school they attended. One teen explained, "I used to smoke pot three times a day in school, just to get through the day. Now I only smoke on the weekend sometimes."

Others have approached North Star staff, asking for help to stop smoking. I now joke that North Star is actually among the three or four "cleanest" groups of school teens in our area, behind only the independent homeschooling groups and one particular private high school.

Managing Behavior

Interested school teachers who visit North Star frequently ask about discipline, as in: Do we have fights and conflicts among the teens? It turns out that I've broken up exactly two fights in my years so far at North Star.

On occasion, we have had teens who bring pocketknives with them to North Star. We require that the knives be kept in bags or pockets unless they are being used for a legitimate purpose, and we allow no fidgeting, flicking, or playing with these items.

I can recall perhaps two instances where a boy, in anger, either flashed his knife or threatened another youth during a conflict with, "I have a knife in my pocket." In these cases, again, the North Star policy is to intervene, send the teen home for violating our expectations, and have meetings with parents to determine what exactly had happened and whether we could restore trust among all parties to maintain a membership at North Star.

Our process for conflict resolution closely matched, and now more intentionally follows, the principles of Restorative Practices. Our Core Staff Member, Joshua Wachtel, brought this vision with him through his work with the International Institute for Restorative Practices, founded by his father, Ted Wachtel. This approach involves asking questions of those involved, such as:

"What happened?"

"What were you thinking at the time?"

"Who has been affected by what you have done?"

"What do you think you need to do to make things right?"

We have found this approach to be especially useful in recent years, in resolving personality conflicts and online bullying that frequently escalate outside of North Star.

We have had teens use social media to send hurtful messages to each other, or about each other. Some have been put-downs, others have encouraged self-harm.

These incidents are harmful to the recipients, who may already be struggling with depression and self-concept, but also angering to parents of both the offender and the victim. We have included teens, parents, and staff together, to resolve these incidents. I've found the question, "What were you thinking at the time?" to be particularly useful when the offender makes an honest attempt to answer it directly to the victim, both sets of parents, and North Star staff.

Usually, we can make good headway in these conversations, and come to terms to restore membership. This year (2018), however, we had a case in which a teen did not want to engage in these conversations, and chose to withdraw from North Star rather than work through their complicated feelings and social relationships.

One of the most difficult moments came in 2007-2008, in our first year at the Russell Street School building. We were all excited to move out of an overcrowded, 2000-square-foot office space into an impressive-looking brick elementary school building, built in 1894 with triple the square footage and many more rooms. At first, we allowed the teen members a full run of the space, to see how the rooms might be used.

Unfortunately, one social group soon "claimed" the music room, settling in first thing in the morning when they arrived. Other members felt unable to use the room for its intended purpose of music-making, and even the Staff Members, including myself, felt like we were intruding when we opened the door or passed through this group. The looks we received from these teens started to feel edgy, even hostile, when we entered the room.

After much conversation with the teens involved, the other members, and at staff meetings, we developed a new rule for North Star. We declared, "All socializing must take place downstairs in the common spaces. The upstairs rooms are reserved for classes, tutoring, and silent reading in the library." Our relations did not end well with these particular teens, but overall, this policy remains in place more than ten years later.

Most teen members at North Star appreciate the fact that this policy is intended to reduce cliques, though we still have some teens who wish they could seclude their small groups into more private spaces than we have to offer. We do have many friendship groups at North Star, and they do find various corners, stairwells, and even kitchen floors to gather around, but the social boundaries of these groups are fluid and overlapping. Of course, teens can also go outside or take themselves for a walk when they want privacy.

We do have conflicts among teens at North Star, but the freedom to move about the building and to come and go at will creates space and control for students that they don't have in schools. Further, our staff has the flexibility to sit in the Common Room, hear the conversations, and intervene actively when we hear negative comments.

Managing teens with clashing personalities is part of our job, but it is often a satisfying bit of work to help teens feel heard, and to resolve their conflicts. One example occurred many years ago, when two young women who had both experienced conflicts with school peers joined North Star. They both were quick to assume others didn't like them and might be scheming against them. These young women also chose to wear mildly revealing clothes, though nothing that merited any kind of intervention.

They were sure other girls were talking about them behind their backs, and tiny interactions about entering a room or sharing a phone could be misconstrued and escalated into nasty comments. We were able to pull the kids involved together in the same room, establish some communication, and defuse the situation. The youth shared some mutual statements of respect and acceptance by the time we were done.

In summary, behavior management and enforcement is a very small part of our world at North Star. Most teens manage themselves quite well. Frequently, I walk into the

Common Room, where perhaps a dozen teens are sitting quietly reading or listening to music with headphones. Just to amuse myself, I say, "Everyone, please calm down."

Many visitors often wonder if we have problems with teens going for walks and bothering the neighbors, or shoplifting from local stores. People fear that unsupervised teens will cause problems. This has not been the case at North Star. In fact, our teens have spent a good deal of money at local convenience stores and pizzerias, and earned the genuine interest of our neighbors.

In our first two locations, we shared our building with other tenants, who often became donors to North Star. In Sunderland, local stores have contributed to fundraisers and raffles. We know the workers by name, and when the isolated problem has arisen, it has been easily resolved. The local police have next to no history of interacting with our teens out in the world during the day.

Joshua and I succeeded in developing a model that allowed us to discard most of the roles we did not like holding as teachers in a junior high school. Our members quickly realize that we are not out to "catch" them doing things wrong, and they begin to relax and explore our environment. They become open to having relationships with adults that are more mature than those they had in school.

The Really Hard Part

We can help teens have an alternative to school, but guess what? Life is still hard. We can't solve all the problems teens and families face.

Some teens arrive at North Star full of enthusiasm and excitement, knowing just how they want to spend their time. They are open to trying things, and they have good relations with their parents. Their families are stable, both emotionally and financially. Even in these seemingly "easy" cases, it can be hard for teens to define and pursue their interests.

Sometimes, they aren't sure what they really want to learn, or if their interests really "count." In our first meetings, teens often think they are supposed to say they are especially interested in whatever school subject has most interested them. They think that homeschooling requires fairly familiar "school-like" academic content. They assume I am expecting this sort of conventional answer, and they expect their parents will require these subjects as part of an agreement to join North Star.

Often, it's hard for a teen to say that their primary interests are not academic at all, but rather something along the lines of a hobby, such as sports, music, or being outdoors. Noah Walker's primary interest was the card game Magic: The Gathering. He was already going to tournaments and winning prize money through the game when he was around 15 years old. As a young adult, he continues attending more competitive and lucrative Magic competitions.

We offered him other classes and tutoring, but we never said, "You know, you shouldn't really keep Magic as your number one priority in life. You'll never be able to make a living from it."

Current member Eliaah Feinstein spends two to four days per week fishing and making videos of his adventures. He has a YouTube channel with hundreds of subscribers, and at age fifteen, he has nearly a dozen corporate sponsors who provide him with all sorts of new equipment for him to feature in his videos.

Eliaah and a friend have been using drones to capture magnificent images of the rivers and geography of their fishing places, including the Deerfield River in western Massachusetts. I'm intending to connect him with the local Chamber of Commerce, which will love using his footage to promote our region. I'm also connecting Eliaah with an older alumnus who is in the filmmaking business, and is seeking a North Star teen apprentice as a way to contribute back to our program.

I was surprised and happy to learn in 2019 that Eliaah is taking two related courses at Greenfield Community College, as a 15-year-old.

We frequently encourage North Star teens feeling stuck to try to find things that interest them out in the world, rather than come to our building every day. One alumnus, Ben Foley, had little interest in our classes and academic offerings when he was twelve and thirteen years old. He enjoyed socializing, but he needed more to do.

I helped him set up an internship with a local baseball team, and his family supported his interest in videography. Ben secured an internship with a local television station, and mastered his skills. He began shooting and editing videos of music concerts. Through his own initiative and audacity, he became the primary videographer and Creative Director for hip-hop artist Mike Stud.

Ben has been living in Los Angeles as a valued and respected member of this team, and he now socializes with many famous people. He also started designing clothes and shoes, and has launched his own brand. At the time of this writing, Ben is a lead creator for football player Johnny Manziel's Comeback SZN store.

In retrospect, Ben needed North Star to get out of school, but he didn't need much else that we offered, except for our ongoing support to trust himself and to take himself seriously. He's now twenty-two and well into a serious professional career. Fortunately, his mother, Jodi Lyn Cutler, has remained involved with North Star, and is now our current Outreach Director.

Devon Kelly-Mott came to North Star after many years of schooling that left her feeling relatively defeated and lost. Devon had a very close relationship with her mother, and she was able to take some unpressured time to consider her options.

Catherine Gobron, our Program Director at that time, developed a close relationship with Devon, and they spent time talking and sharing interests. Catherine introduced Devon to a North Star parent for an herbalism internship, opening up a new world for her. Devon also took her first community college class, belly dancing, with great joy and success.

Devon used these positive relationships with adults to validate herself and imagine a future centered on these fresh interests. Devon ultimately graduated from Greenfield Community College and then Warren Wilson College in Asheville, North Carolina. She is now a model and an entrepreneur, whose business is called Apothefaerie: Wildcrafted Wonders and Potent Potions.

Helping teens discover their interests and establish their own goals may sound relatively simple, but it was and is not. When teens don't know what they want to do with their time, our culture generally demands that adults fill it with requirements and structured activities, until the teen can make some declaration. North Star's approach of sitting with teens and waiting for inspiration to arrive is relatively rare.

We support and prioritize hobbies that schools frequently discount or ignore. Parents worry, and the teens themselves worry, "When will I care about something? When will I get a life?" We can't offer answers, but we can offer a strategy: Relax, wonder, take a risk, and care.

Mental and Physical Health

Even in the best of circumstances, cheerfully building a new schedule and routine can be a daunting prospect.

As I've already mentioned, some teens arrive at North Star with some anxiety or depression. Our approach opens things up for these young people, but it hardly "solves" the problem.

Teens with anxiety find it hard to leave their houses to come to North Star; or, when they arrive, they may hover by the door outside and find it hard to come inside. We have watched some teens walk laps around the building, unable to enter.

One member took months to go from "officially joining" to "showing up." The thought of coming to North Star was paralyzing. Happily, he finally developed a plan to come for just one or two hours per day to participate in one class and speak to a couple of teens for a few minutes in the Common Room. As each day went well, we could see the change in his demeanor. Still, this process required patience and acceptance by our staff that most schools find difficult to provide.

Teens with depression often wake up feeling bleak. They may not want to face a new community or new expectations. In fact, they may feel that they are about to ruin this new opportunity, too. "I can't even not go to school," has been a thought that freezes some of our members.

Some teens struggle with sleep disorders, migraines, and other health issues that make attending North Star very difficult. We can help these families escape from the negative spiral of missing school and facing make-up work, but we can't do much about these primary problems. This year in particular, we have had mixed results. One member with a chronic sleep problem has been unable to come to North Star more than a handful of days over the past two years, and North Star's role in her life is rather marginal.

Another teen has yet to join, but her story bears mentioning here. She has been missing school due to her migraines, and has tried more than two dozen medications. She spends lots of her time at doctor appointments. Her make-up work for school has piled up into a mountain of stress, which unfortunately seems to contribute further to her health woes.

I've met with this family just once, and encouraged them to submit a homeschooling plan, which would eliminate the school part of her problem. In a follow-up conversation, the mother was exhilarated. "We went and filed the homeschooling plan, just like you coached us. It was so empowering! She really wants to start at North Star, but just can't do it yet. You'll see us eventually." The mother reported that the daughter has plenty of interests, and has no trouble replacing her pile of make-up work with other work, including some studies of basic health and brain anatomy. Perhaps this girl will join North Star next year.

A true highlight of the past three years has been supporting a healthy lifestyle for Kim Chin-Gibbons. Kim has sleep issues, and found school exhausting. Almost any major family event or personal activity led her to miss school the following day. She, too, was plagued with make-up work that tended to make things worse, not better.

Once she started homeschooling, each day was a cautious experiment. At first, Kim came to North Star sparingly, arranging to show up only for certain hours or certain classes. Our role was to welcome and encourage, not to push.

This approach worked well for Kim. She quickly became a mainstay in the North Star Band, and she started another band with North Star members and friends. She also refined her skills as a photographer, and she has created a stunning collection of portraits and other images.

She has photographed North Star events, and shared her insights as a photography tutor with other North Star teens. She has merged her photography and musical interests by taking photos of local music performers in concert, and has an impressive portrait portfolio to show for it.

Outside of North Star, she has volunteered with a local concert series, and is now interning with Double Edge Theatre, an innovative acrobatic theater company. She is also involved with the Institute for Musical Arts, a summer rock-and-roll music camp for girls. Kim is also a core participant in People to Watch: The Next Generation, a teen group promoting local emerging artists in a variety of genres.

By 2018, she came to North Star nearly every day, frequently in the mornings. In addition to practicing and performing music here, Kim teaches guitar to other North Star members. She attends numerous classes and has sought relationships with many Staff Members. She always has a smile and a welcome for visitors and new members.

Three years into her North Star experience, Kim's life is full to the point of overflowing. She stays home whenever she and her parents determine she needs a personal day of rest. Does this story really belong in this chapter as a hard case? In retrospect, perhaps not, as Kim and her parents have used self-directed learning as the means to take charge of constructing and managing an appropriate schedule.

North Star provided vision, support, and community. We did not provide medical advice or directly intervene on Kim's sleep issues. I think it is fair to conclude that Kim's case was a hard case for her and her parents, and an inspiring one for North Star staff.

Resistance

I frequently meet teens who have stopped trying in school, and who resist cooperating with teachers and parents. Only rarely do I meet students who are acting out and causing mayhem in schools. Usually I meet teens who refuse to do their work, accept "F" grades, and suffer all the consequences their parents can impose on them for this behavior. Sometimes, these teens refuse to get out of bed or leave their rooms in the morning, or refuse to enter the school when delivered there by their parents.

These teens have developed some compelling need to prove to themselves that they will not allow themselves to be forced or coerced into doing things that they don't want to do. They are often surprised at our initial meetings when I tell them that I won't try to make them do anything. They've never encountered a "school" like this before.

Nevertheless, the entry ticket to North Star, if teens are under age 16, is having their parents develop a home-schooling plan for their local superintendent. The parents want and need the teen to commit to a set of activities they can write up with some degree of integrity to present to the school office.

This is where things can break down. Teens won't agree to anything ahead of time. They tell their parents, "Write whatever you want. I'll do it if I feel like it." The parents, teen, and I sit around a table looking at each other, wondering if any resolution is possible.

Many times, our process ends at this juncture without the teen joining North Star. Either they stay in school, or the family finds another school that satisfies the parents' needs to see their child have solid requirements.

Many parents sympathize with their children in this position. They question both the rigid content and the controlling atmosphere of school, and they understand their children's resistance. They may wish their kids could just go along with the system like "normal" kids, but they understand the problem from their children's point of view. The parents also may feel they have hit a dead end, trying to force their teens to conform to their school, and they are ready for a change.

Unfortunately, this show of parental support and understanding doesn't always bring the teen around. At one of our most memorable "Beginning of the Year" meetings, one such resistant teen faced a couple of North Star staff and parents. When we asked him, rather innocently, "So, what are some of your goals for this year?" he felt cornered and on the spot.

He looked up at us, with anger and frustration growing inside of him. He suddenly stood up, shouted, "Fuck you!" and walked out of the building. The adults looked at each other, a bit stunned, and finally said, "Well, I guess we'll have to try this meeting again, another day."

This teen really wanted to be a member of North Star, but could not bring himself to announce his goals to all of us. All of us—the boy, the parent, the grandparent, the North Star staff—knew that North Star would be the best option available, and we avoided putting him on the spot again in that way.

Fortunately, the young man could acknowledge that he very much wanted to be a member of North Star. He was willing to interact with the staff, and consider some exploratory activities. He particularly liked some building and woodworking opportunities one of our Staff Members provided for him. Some of these were one-on-one projects, and others were formal jobs that the part-time Staff

Member did for work on days he wasn't at North Star.

The hero of this story, for me, turned out to be the young man's grandmother. Her daughter—the boy's mother—had recently died from an illness. The boy was angry at his father, his stepfather, and the world in general. His grandmother stood by him, and provided unconditional support and love throughout these years. She supported his choice to live with a friend's family, and she provided logistical and financial support for everyone engaged with her grandson. All of us, including the teen, celebrated her role in his life.

It turns out that this young man went on to a very productive, three-year tenure at North Star, in which he developed very close relationships with some of the staff. He became a building apprentice with one Staff Member, and he is now a professional carpenter as an adult.

Frequently, we face the stalemate of parents requiring a minimal amount of academic work, and a teen flat-out refusing to do anything based on an arbitrary requirement. We do our best to facilitate a solution: Either the teen can agree to do something to recognize the parents' need for some output, or the parents can let go of this demand and see if they can live with the feeling of being "irresponsible parents."

The truth is, we rarely solve this problem satisfactorily. If we are unable to defuse this tension early on, and cannot achieve parents and children recognizing each other's needs and feeling somehow that they are on the same team, we usually see the child return to school within a matter of months. In our very first year, we had one of our most difficult cases like this, which has informed my approach ever since.

Marta MacRostie was a fiercely independent teen, who had no desire to accommodate schoolwork she considered meaningless. She was an artist, a musician, and an activist.

Her parents were academic sorts, who wanted her to get a "good education." They differed on their vision for homeschooling, and we had many meetings in which Marta simply refused to do the sort of work her parents demanded.

They would tell each other, in front of me, "I love you, but I can't go along with what you want."

The situation escalated when Marta's parents re-enrolled her in school and she refused to attend. The social workers from the Department of Social Services showed up, and Marta was threatened with being removed from her home if she didn't start going to school according to her parents' wishes.

In the end, Marta started attending school, but she refused to participate in the classes and withdrew as soon as she legally could.

Her family's loving relationships transcended this episode, but the whole procedure showed me just how things can play out when the conflict escalates. I generally felt like a failure, and have tried to head off these situations since then.

The good news is that Marta has proceeded to have an artistic career, including a college degree from the University of Massachusetts, and a life as a professional puppeteer.

Transience

The overall transience at North Star is a hard part of the job. Sometimes, members arrive at ages 11-13 years old, and stay for five to seven years. But for the most part, even when things go well, many teens are members for just two to four years. When things go poorly, they are members for only a matter of months.

This freedom to move on from North Star—whether because one is ready for young adulthood, or because one chooses to return to school—is part of the landscape we have created for ourselves.

During our first couple of years, I was surprised and discouraged to see teens move on from North Star so quickly. I have learned, though, that everyone ages out!

When a mature seventeen-year-old moves on to community college, a part-time job, and some travel opportunities, North Star has to celebrate another success story. When a youth says, "Thank you, but I believe I'll do better for myself back in a school program," the only appropriate response is to admire the self-assessment and wish them well.

I've discovered over the years, in many ways, that teens retain the memory of being a North Star member long after they have left our program. Many encourage their siblings or family friends to join North Star. Others show up years later, seeking to volunteer in order to "give something back" to North Star. Many call or write to North Star staff, seeking some sort of recommendation for a job or other special opportunity. Many alumni show up at our parties, fundraisers, and special events.

When I call or send email through the alumni list every year or two, to update the alumni database, I find that many teens who had relatively brief tenures at North Star are surprisingly happy to be counted as alumni and are glad to catch up with me about our lives. They are curious to hear how things are going at North Star.

I feel I have had more meaningful relationships with even the relatively short-term members of North Star than those I experienced with students as an eighth grade history teacher.

What Keeps Me Going

The hard parts of North Star are difficult. Many times I feel we are facing the same issues year after year.

What keeps me going is that we regularly receive appreciation from our members. Sometimes we get this news indirectly, such as in a parent report to the Superintendent about the progress of their child during the past year. In the summer of 2018, one family asked me to review a letter before they submitted it, and the over-all scope of the letter really made my day, and offers an example of what's in this work for the staff.

Alyssa Zagorin came to North Star in the fall of 2017, 13 years old and somewhat shut down to life. She was refusing to go to school, and losing interest for some of her longstanding pursuits, such as writing and physical exercise.

Alyssa is a particularly strong-willed individual, and her parents (a teacher and a musician) were not sure how much to push or fight about various behaviors. They were worried that their child was not going to school, and they were even more concerned that she sometimes resisted even coming out of her bedroom.

The North Star approach seemed to offer some immediate relief, as at least they wouldn't have to fight about school for the rest of the year. Still, there were expectations and agreements about getting out of the house, attending North Star, and doing some academic work that Alyssa might or might not honor.

In her first weeks at North Star, Alyssa behaved somewhat cautiously towards the staff and the community. I wasn't entirely sure how things would proceed, though I found myself quite supportive of Alyssa's resistance to doing things that she wasn't entirely sure came from her own motivation. Metaphorically, it was as if she was cleaning out her closet completely before she could agree to put anything back in, with no definite promises.

In what now feels like a relatively short set of weeks, Alyssa determined that North Star was trustworthy, and that she had many interests worthy of pursuing: writing, exercise, photography, pit bull dogs, and her extended family relationships, among others. By the middle of the year, she was fully engaged at North Star, both with staff and teens. She even participated in several of our monthly Information Sessions, telling her story to visitors.

Following is her parents' summary of the year. Please read it with your own comparison to what a likely outcome of staying in eighth grade might have been for Alyssa. For me, the difference between the real summary and imaginary school outcome is what keeps me going.

Dr. Michael Morris, Superintendent of Schools

Dear Dr. Morris,

We write to update you on our experience home-schooling our child, Alyssa. Our home-based education continues through the summer in a relaxed fashion, and we are making plans for September.

Alyssa invested considerable time reading, tackling a number of substantial books. Titles she read include: The Hate You Give, Angie Thomas; Ninth Ward, Jewell Parker Rhodes; The Border, Steve Schafer: Riding Freedom, Pam Ryan; Adultolescence, Gabbie Hanna; Bad Blood, Jennifer Lynn Barnes; I Know Why the Caged Bird Sings, Maya Angelou; and Romeo and Juliet, William Shakespeare (studied in multiple ways: original annotated text, filmed adaptations, age-appropriate abridgement.)

Alyssa entered into homeschooling intending to work on fiction writing. She'd already begun a young adult novel, subsequently completing about 70 pages. She also engaged in a number of writing-related classes and activities at North Star, and also tried her hand at writing short stories.

Alyssa used the online resource Khan Academy to work on her math skills. She focused on revisiting and strengthening areas of weakness, to be better prepared for Algebra.

For Science this year, Alyssa used a variety of book and online resources. She explored an interest in the astronomy of the solar system, researching and preparing presentations on the planets Jupiter and Saturn. She also studied psychology, through her own reading and through activities at North Star. One area of focus was the influence of heredity on personality and character traits, studied by reading and discussing literature on twin studies. Alyssa also learned about the scientific classification of plants, in addition to which she participated in a North Star class that involved volunteer work at a farm. Alyssa also learned about balanced nutrition and human health, through a North Star class that involved planning and preparing nutritious meals. Alyssa also explored an interest in dogs, dog breeding, and dog behavior, through a mix of reading, online learning, and discussion with North Star staff.

Alyssa spent time learning about topics of interest in the realm of Social Studies. She did some reading on immigration, and followed debates on immigration policies as current events. Alyssa became interested in learning about the foster care system. She researched laws and policies in the Commonwealth of Massachusetts regulating foster care. She researched differences and similarities in foster care systems among a number of states.

Alyssa discovered and explored a new interest in Dramatic Performance this spring, something which in earlier years was a source of anxiety for her. She engaged in a Comedy Improvisation workshop at North Star, in which she worked not just on delivering comedy but on performing in public, as well.

Alyssa also took part in several other classes at North Star not mentioned above, including Sex Ed and Herbalism.

Alyssa has a burgeoning interest in Photography. She looks for unusual angles in composition, tending to focus on objects and landscapes. She likes to focus on interesting textures, and finding ways to highlight the texture of an object against the back-

ground of the photo. She tried to take the time to notice things that people would normally walk by, and make those the focus of her images. Alyssa created an Instagram channel dedicated to displaying these photos.

Alyssa was engaged in physical training and athletics through the year. She and her father lifted weights three times weekly, and in doing this Alyssa learned safe and proper methods for basic barbell lifts, such as the low-bar squat, deadlift, overhead press, and bench press. During the spring, she began to participate in a weekly Roller Derby training program for teens at Pioneer Roller Derby in Florence, which she will continue to do through the summer. During the summer, Alyssa will continue to do Roller Derby and strength-training, and will also do regular aerobic conditioning in preparation for participating in the 7th-8th grade Suburban Youth Football League on the Amherst Hurricanes.

Alyssa got her first paid job this year, doing occasional mother's helper work for a neighbor with 3- and 6-year-old children.

Alyssa and her father engaged in a home project to finish a basement room to be a 'hang-out' space. Alyssa learned many basic carpentry and construction skills. She used her knowledge of math when learning how to measure and plan. She learned the safe use of basic tools. She learned how to work with wood framing stock and wall-finishing panels, and to use a variety of fasteners to fix them in their proper places. Alyssa spent many weekend afternoons on this project, and she and her father expect to finish it over the summer. Alyssa put her developing 'fix-it' skills to use at North Star, when she volunteered to do a number of small repair jobs around the premises, including fixing a door that wasn't hanging straight.

Alyssa made gains in her social life this year. In the educational realm, Alyssa settled into the environment at North Star very well, attending classes and activities four times a week. North Star staff report that she developed good friendships with a number of her peers, and that she is growing in her abilities to take risks in learning, which allows her to participate in learning in a group setting much more effectively. Staff also tell us that Alyssa developed a reputation as a student who engages with peers and curriculum, and is helpful and empathic to others.

Alyssa's success engaging in homeschooling, including her activities at North Star, greatly reduced her overall stress level, and Alyssa made social gains outside of school as well.

We plan to continue homeschooling with Alyssa next year as well, which would be eighth grade. Looking ahead, she is currently excited about continuing to explore Photography and writing. We will keep you posted about her progress. Other goals this coming year include continuing with math into Geometry, building on her essay writing skills, and studying Spanish.

Thanks for your support,

Amy Rose and Neil Zagorin
July 5, 2018

Summary

In most of this book—and actually, in most of my life—I have tried to focus on the positive, and to provide leadership to the North Star community. For the most part, I find it rather easy to be positive, because I have created the organization to fit my own vision and inclinations. I have a lot of flexibility to choose the tasks and the work that most appeal to me. I consider myself lucky to be able to look forward to going to work, and to feel that

I'm making a difference in people's lives. I'm optimistic that I can share some of our work in a way that positively influences others and will have a constructive impact on our wider society.

Still, there are challenges. Most of the challenges I have described in this chapter have solid rewards for those addressing and resolving them.

Every program that works with young people faces many of these issues, and just about every small, innovative, private school or non-profit program struggles to meet a budget. Having serious budget worries and dealing with hard cases come with the territory North Star has claimed for itself. Shifting an educational program into a student-as-customer model poses some unique situations, but most private schools and summer camps face the same situations.

The purpose of this chapter is to describe some of the worries, frustrations, and hardships that are part of running this sort of program. At North Star, we've pretty much figured out our responses as we've gone along, and I value the camaraderie of the Staff and Board, who have supported me over all these years.

In my consulting with people interested in replicating our model, I try to convey that the job is not "all fun, all the time." Running a small non-profit is hard work, and doing so when the program is unfamiliar and confusing to the general public makes it a bit harder yet.

Nevertheless, I have never thought twice about my choice to take on these challenges. In this way, I align myself with the North Star members who leave schooling to take on self-directed learning, confront the difficult aspects of the process, and emerge with some lifelong perspective about independence and empowerment. It seems like a healthy way to live.

Overall, I feel I have traded the security of school teaching for the freedom and stress of running a small business. We see our students and families as customers. The hard parts of the job described in this chapter are real, but

I'm fairly certain that other than the financial stress of keeping North Star afloat, I've carried far less stress with me over the years than I carried when I was a schoolteacher.

10

Alumni Outcomes

How could we be so confident that respecting teens' freedom and accepting "no" for an answer was such a good idea? What was the evidence? A few good stories from Grace Llewellyn? John Holt's philosophy? A handful of other books on homeschooling and unschooling? Meeting with a few local teens who had pursued this approach and turned out more or less okay?

In truth, there wasn't a lot of data to go on. Overall, not much research on the impact of homeschooling and unschooling had been done when we started Pathfinder. What the heck were we doing?

Well, the truth is, Joshua and I never harbored a moment of doubt about the approach. We knew that our school teaching wasn't serving very many of our students effectively. At most, only about a third of the students in our school were on the honor roll, receiving the official message that they were "good students," worthy of praise.

Many of these students achieved their good grades with a large degree of stress and anxiety. Among the minority of high-achievers who did so relatively calmly, only a handful found their learning to be useful and satisfying. And, then, within this tiny handful of successful, stress-free students happy about their learning, nearly all of them wanted more time for their own hobbies. All of them preferred summer time and vacation to school. All of them rooted for snow days.

Readers may find this conclusion a bit too cynical, but it really is an accurate depiction of how I felt about teaching in school: Few students really wanted to be there. As I hope I have made clear in earlier chapters, that wasn't good enough for me. I wanted to create a place where people wanted to be, where they would be rooting against snow days. (This would become one way I have always measured North Star's success: The teens respond to our snow day announcements with sad faces.)

We weren't worried that providing an option to traditional school for our students who were largely "going through the motions" was likely to be a bad thing. Further, we did believe the stories we read in the homeschooling literature. We had been inspired by the people we met, who were the homeschooling pioneers of the 1980s and 1990s.

We had contacted colleges and universities to understand the admissions process for homeschoolers, and we knew there were no obstacles. We understood how self-directed learners moved on to jobs, training programs, and entrepreneurship with (and without) GEDs, instead of traditional high school diplomas. We were positive there were no serious risks to exploring life without school.

More than two decades later, a review of our alumni and their lifelong experiences allows for a simple conclusion: We were right.

I offer this conclusion out of respect for the process, not from a sense of self-aggrandizement. Since the origination and expansion of compulsory schooling, many other writers and school critics have offered this insight: that people can thrive without, or in spite of, completing high school. North Star is one specific approach to proving this point.

We who have worked with teens at North Star knew that our students were thriving, but we wanted quantitative data about what happened to our alumni, to prove it to others. In 2017, I released a review of North Star's alumni experiences through the Alliance for Self-Directed Education. I'll include some of the highlights in this chapter. Then I will discuss some of the findings in a study by North Star alumna Emily Odgers, who conducted her research in 2016-2017, as part of her senior year Capstone

Project at Warren Wilson College. I will conclude the chapter with some further thoughts about alumni, especially the now-adult alumni from our first years.

What Happens to Self-Directed Learners?

I began the Alliance review by sharing my preference for using anecdotes, rather than quantitative data, to tell the North Star story. We do not have data such as test scores, grade point averages, or easily counted items. We aren't sure whether the number of alumni who obtained a GED is newsworthy, as many of our members did not perceive it as a major goal and moved on to private colleges or jobs without this document.

The qualitative data is difficult, too, for me. I start with the concern that we have no "controls." A teen could not both stay in school and experiment with North Star. The qualitative data about self-esteem, satisfaction with the experience, or emotional health would be largely self-reported. I wasn't confident that the effort to collect the data would be worth much to those who wanted evidence.

Fortunately, some friends from the University of Massachusetts School of Education and at The Alliance for Self-Directed Education persuaded me that we could tell an interesting story with the basic information we already possessed. In the introduction to the report, I listed their questions: "What brought our members to North Star? What did our alumni do when they first left? And after that, what were their second, third, and fourth activities after leaving North Star?"

I conceded that answering those questions was possible, and that, in fact, it would be rather fun for me to collect the information. I have stayed in touch with many alumni, and this project would give me a good reason to reach out to everyone who had been a member.

The project involved efforts to discover the post-North Star activities of 473 alumni. When I was struggling to compile the data in a meaningful way, Peter Gray, author of *Free to Learn* and founding member

of the Alliance for Self-Directed Education, suggested dividing the story into parts:
1) North Star alumni who moved on from North Star to college, work, or other post-high school opportunities, and
2) North Star alumni who returned to middle school or high school when they left North Star.

This helpful suggestion formed the skeleton for the report in its final form.

In the Introduction to the article, I reported a few findings about the full set of 473 alumni, including this gem:

North Star coaches teens to leave school and embark on a self-directed path. It turns out that for eighty-two percent of our members, the first activity after North Star is: school. This includes young teens that return to high school and older teens that go on to community college, four-year college, or formal certificate or training programs. In the long-term, at least sixty-nine percent of North Star alumni enroll in a college or formal training program.

How about that? For all of our philosophy and hard work teaching youth that school is optional, what do the vast majority of our members do, immediately upon leaving North Star? They go to school. Whether it's a return to middle school or high school, or on to community college, four-year college, or a formal training program of some kind, North Star members return to our mainstream culture's pursuit of education.

I hope this number allays the fears of those who imagine North Star to be some sort of anarchist cult, deterring children from ever participating in common civic culture in the future.

North Star is clearly one place, one approach that some families use in figuring out how to support their children in growing up as happy and capable young people. When things go well, they stay for several years. When they do not, they return to school. In either case, the goal for most North Star members is to attend college or formal training of some kind.

For the eighteen percent of members whose first post-North Star activity is not school, we know that most enter the workforce. Some of these workers are self-employed. Some are craftspeople or artists. Many of them eventually enroll in college after some time working.

Indeed, a small handful of North Star alumni have not ever returned to school and have not found sustained employment. Even in these cases, many teens report that their years at North Star were the best years of their adolescence.

Part One:
Moving on From North Star to Young Adulthood
This section of the report looked at the 267 alumni who moved on to college, work, or other opportunities in the adult world after their time at North Star. We found that seventy-two percent chose college or a training program as their first activity, with twenty-eight percent choosing some form of work or unusual experience, such as travel. At least eighty-one percent of these alumni eventually enrolled in college or training programs, though that number will increase as some recent alumni who started with work eventually decide to attend college or training programs as they grow older.

These percentages for college enrollment exceed state and national averages. Opting out of high school in a positive way with the support of North Star does not leave students excluded from higher education. In fact, it is likely that the confidence in their ability to learn, which they develop at North Star, motivates them to further their education.

Among the students who have chosen work, at least twenty-seven percent report some period of being self-employed or pursuing some unusual opportunity. We don't have a way to compare that percentage to traditional high school graduates, but this data suggests that North Star alumni may continue in the spirit of self-direction when they move on from our program.

While researching outcomes, we also assigned Intake Categories to all of these alumni, with the intention of generating more specific data about how teens do, based on their status when they joined North Star. The report reads:

> For Intake, we have two questions. First, at the time of joining, was the teen coming from a "School," or were they already legally "Homeschooling?" Second, how were they doing in this prior situation?
>
> Our goal to have a relatively small, but inclusive, set of presenting categories has led to: "Managing Well," "Mental Health Issues," "Resisting or Refusing," and "Major Learning Differences or Physical Health Issues."
>
> We recognize the arbitrary and limiting nature of labeling in this way, but for the sake of the project, we feel reasonably comfortable with this manner of describing our population. These intake categories have been assigned by current and former Staff Members, based on our memories. As of 2015, we have begun assigning categories at the time each member joins.
>
> **Intake Data for 267 Alumni Who Moved On to Young Adult Activities**
>
> **Activity Prior to North Star:**
>
> Enrolled in school: 76%
>
> Independently Homeschooling: 24%
>
> **Intake Category:**
>
> Managing Well: 58%
>
> Refusing or Resisting School: 22%

Mental Health Issues: 16%

Major Learning Differences or Health Issues: 4%

 I find this chart a wonderful numerical summary of my career. More than three-quarters of this group left school with North Star's support. A solid majority of these teens were Managing Well, meaning that without North Star, they most likely would have continued through high school and graduated in the regular way.

 Here's how we defined the Intake Categories:

Managing Well in School or Independent Homeschooling (58%): These youth are doing well in their current setting, but are seeking more freedom and support to pursue their interests. In school, these teens may be on the honor roll, attend regularly, and have few discipline problems. Their main complaint is feeling bored in school or not having enough time outside of school to pursue their interests. In a homeschooling setting, these teens are thriving, but investigating North Star as a potential addition to their routine and seeking a larger social community.

Refusing or Resisting in School or as an Independent Homeschooler
(22%): These teens have stopped trying to succeed in school. They may have stopped attending, or are skipping days on a regular basis. In school, they are refusing to do homework. Sometimes they are acting out and developing a negative behavior record. As homeschoolers, they experience conflict with their parents about basic family expectations.

Mental Health Issues in School or as an Independent Homeschooler
(16%): These youth are struggling with conditions such as anxiety or depression. They may be self-harming, and sometimes suicidal. They may feel bullied and unsafe due to past experiences. In school, these teens are not attend-

ing regularly due to these issues and find that missing school adds additional anxiety and tension to their lives. As homeschoolers, they are having difficulty getting out of the house and sustaining any progress with hobbies and interests.

Major Learning Difference or Health Problems
(4%): A small group of teens arrive at North Star without fitting into any of the above categories. The most common reason is they have some physical health disease or condition that is making regular attendance and participation in school or homeschooling impossible, despite the teen's desire to succeed. One common example is sleep disorder. Also, North Star has had several members diagnosed to be on the autism spectrum, which best fits in this category.

In my 2015 speech for Thrive 2020 in Guernsey, England, I described three students as examples of our alumni, one for each of the three main categories. For Managing School, I told the story of Oliver Spiro, who came to North Star out of sixth grade. He was doing just fine, though he was generally bored and underwhelmed by his classroom learning.

His mother called North Star, seeking some after-school enrichment for him. Though we offered some of what she was looking for, she was confused about the fact that North Star was an "instead-of-school" program, not an after-school program. Regardless, Oliver joined, stayed a member for five years, went on to double-major in Mathematics and Chinese at the University of Massachusetts Honors Program, and is now professionally employed.

Laura Ross has told her story many times, and she remains a spectacular example of a teen overcoming anxiety and mental health issues. She had excelled in school through eighth grade, when she developed some health and anxiety issues that made being inside the school building feel impossible for her. After some back-and-forth with independent homeschooling, school, and North Star, Laura joined North Star and settled into a serious academic program.

She came to North Star only for tutorials with staff for

three years, before she had an epiphany and decided she could do classes with peers. Laura helped organize and teach a class at North Star, attended several others, and joined me on several panel presentations, including one as a keynote speaker at the AERO Conference, and for the Compass Program in Ottawa.

Laura became involved in the wider community as well, as a member of a rock band. She also taught guitar lessons to younger girls. Laura graduated from Mount Holyoke College in 2018, with a degree in Astronomy. She is now exploring interests in health and nursing through a position at a birthing clinic. Her self-paced resolution of her anxiety issues while pursuing serious academics and music is compelling.

Jonah Meyer came to North Star in 2006, as a stereotypical "wild child" at age 13. He hated school and resisted it for all he was worth. His academically inclined parents were deeply worried, but they saw no point in enrolling Jonah in middle school. During his time at North Star, Jonah became an avid rock climber. He became interested in the North Star model and read at least twenty-five books from my John Holt and alternative education classics shelf.

He decided he had things to say, and helped edit North Star's newsletter. He took two chemistry classes at the University of Massachusetts, and at age 17, completed Greenfield Community College's intensive Outdoor Leadership Program. He then worked three years for the State of Connecticut, in an outdoor education program for troubled teens.

Jonah is now roaming the world, rock climbing and considering his next steps. The past ten years have been an extraordinarily positive adventure for Jonah and his family, and it's hard to imagine what Jonah's life would be like now, had he been forced to stay in school.

I want to mention that Jonah's younger sister, India, also joined North Star, but as a young woman who was managing well in school. She saw the freedom her brother lived with, and she wanted the same opportunity. In

Jonah's words, "India did everything I did, but she was better at everything."

India spent two years at North Star, worked at the local rock-climbing gym, completed the Outdoor Leadership Program, became an EMT, and now lives and works in Utah.

Among the four percent of teens who don't fall into any of the above categories, a fine example is Fares Croteau, who could be an alumnus, but is returning in 2018 for a seventh year on a limited basis.

Fares came to North Star in 2013, utterly worn down by his schooling experience. He and his family really wanted school to work. They tried for years to work within the system to have Fares make the most of his opportunities, and Fares tried his best. He was not resisting, he was not plagued with mental health issues, but he did have some learning differences that made school difficult for him.

His father Chris wrote for our newsletter, "I'll admit I was out of ideas, just about at my wit's end...My son Fares may just be the most caring, lovable, and thoughtful human being, ever...it was very apparent to me that school could be overwhelming."

Chris recalls that Fares developed a speech impediment, and was diagnosed with dyspraxia. Fares tried to do well in school, but he remembers, "In other schools I have attended (before North Star), I felt very tired and insecure. Sometimes I just felt defeated, and nothing made sense to me. I just wanted to go home. I felt frustrated with how many of my teachers were very impatient. I couldn't keep up and contribute fast enough."

I remember his arrival as being marked by a painfully revealing anecdote:

During one of his first visits here, Fares was involved in some outdoor play with other teens. When Chris came to pick him up, he told me, "I was driving down the road and saw some kids running. I thought to myself, 'Oh, that's surprising, another kid here has the same shirt as Fares.'"

Chris hadn't seen his son running and playing in a group in such a long time, that he just assumed the child in the shirt must be someone else.

Fares has become the heart and soul of North Star over the past six years. He frequently stops me just to say, "Ken, thank you for starting North Star!" or, "Ken, you are really great!" I take it personally, but I will add that Fares offers these affirmations regularly to many staff and teens at North Star.

Fares has literally made himself the life of the party, as he initiates events such as North Star's Halloween Ball, Winter Dance, and the hosting of our region's Pride Prom in June. Fares loves music, and he especially loves sharing his favorite songs as the DJ at these events. He also plays guitar and sings in North Star's rock band.

Over the past couple of years, Fares has been a central part of a team fostering local youth bands in our region, called People to Watch: The Next Generation. Fares may well become a concert promoter, in addition to some sort of musician or social host. As he reduces his time at North Star, he will be experimenting with community college and work. We are all curious to see what he chooses to do.

In the newsletter, Chris celebrated: "The sense of empowerment, the sense of relief I felt taking my child, my sweet beautiful child, out of the system that never worked for him, is one of the few truly great milestones of my life. North Star instilled hope in the midst of immense emotional frustration."

Fares summarizes, "Knowing that people really care about me and what I am doing makes me want to engage more. I've opened up a lot. I have some wonderful friends. North Star is like a big family, a big family that occasionally plays dodgeball with stuffed animals."

Part Two: Return to School or Independent Homeschooling
Here's the introduction to this section of the report:

When Joshua Hornick and I created North Star back in 1996, we imagined we would be supporting teens to leave school and embark on the journey of self-directed learning. We had read The Teenage Liberation Handbook: How to Quit School and Get a Real Life and Education *by Grace Llewellyn, and we expected to coach teens to move through North Star and on to college, work, and other young adult adventures.*

From the very first year, however, we saw the use of North Star to be more varied and complicated. It turned out that every year, some of the members that we had inspired to try living and learning without school would leave North Star and return to high school.

As the years mounted, we began to realize that this short-term use of North Star was a genuine pattern for a solid number of teens. We also saw that some teens left North Star to become independent homeschoolers, or to resume an independent homeschooling experience they had enjoyed prior to joining our program.

During the early years, as the first teens informed me of their plans to return to school, I confess to feeling some disappointment. Were we failing these members? Were they leaving us with anger or frustration?

We were not collecting data about their reasons for returning to school, but over time, I have come to understand this choice as a natural part of our work. Some teens just want a year out of school during the middle school years as a "gap year" before high school. Others become curious about what a different school has to offer, whether it's the public high school of the system they left, a charter school, or a private school. Some want the high school experience of academic classes, sports, and proms. Some want to prove to themselves that they can handle this world in a way they could not before.

In 2012, I wrote an article for the *Huffington Post* titled, "Eighth Grade Out!" celebrating this use of North Star. I would love to see this phrase become a familiar sub-set of "The Gap Year" lexicon.

This alumni study offered me the opportunity to re-connect with many students who used North Star in this way, and the conversations were touching. Many of these young people told me that the year out of school mattered immensely to them. I included one such note in the report, from Clare Ryan:

A quick sketch of my recent career: I graduated from Yale Law School in 2013. I spent the 2013-2014 academic year teaching in the Political Science department at Macalester. I spent 2014-2015 as a human rights fellow at the European Court of Human Rights in Strasbourg, France. Now, I am a law clerk on the Ninth Circuit Court of Appeals in San Diego, CA. I was admitted to the MA bar, although I haven't actually practiced law there.

I'm not sure what's next exactly, but I've loved the adventure so far! Honestly, I wouldn't have had the confidence and motivation to do half of these things if it hadn't been for my year at North Star (Pathfinder – at the time). That year was absolutely transformative and I would be happy to talk to interested kids or families about it, if that would ever be helpful to you.

I have come to value offering teens a one- or two-year respite from school, and then supporting them to return to high school by their own choice. I'm also inspired by those teens who left school with our support, then realized that they did not need or want a North Star membership to pursue their learning. These teens moved right along to independent homeschooling, and I rejoice in their freedom and success.

Summary of the Alumni Report

This report offered me a way to describe and categorize North Star alumni experiences, and make a reasonably interesting argument that North Star has a generally positive influence on its members. There is much more to delve into here, with closer examinations of post-North Star activities by each intake category, and by considering the alumni outcomes of other Liberated Learners centers (see Chapter 9) using our model. I expect to focus on this sort of analysis in the future.

Unschooling Unpacked:
Outcomes of a Self-Directed Learning Community

Emily Odgers was a member of North Star in 2010-2011. After living and working in Washington, D.C., Emily enrolled at Warren Wilson College in Asheville, North Carolina, from which she graduated in 2017. For her Capstone Project, Emily chose to do a qualitative study of North Star alumni. She wanted to measure "...the social and educational outcomes of North Star alumni, while also considering how unschoolers perceive their experiences during and after North Star."

Emily took a list of 301 North Star alumni from 1996-2010, and emailed a survey to a random sample of 150 individuals from among them. She got 53 responses, a 36.3% response rate. She followed up with eleven of these respondents for more extensive interviews.

There was genuine randomness to this process, though limited by the fact that North Star does not have current contact information for all alumni, and that participation in the survey and interviews was self-selective. Nevertheless, I did not hand-pick these alumni for Emily, and they remain anonymous to me. Here are some of Emily's findings:

Education and Income
- "Though the sample size is relatively small for any conclusive findings, it appears that alumni of North Star are more highly educated than the average U.S. adult."
- "North Star alumni who attended college reported high rates of academic achievement, with the significant majority of college graduates, seventy-six percent, reporting having a final cumulative GPA of 3.6 to 4.0 and above. Therefore, North Star alumni appear to not only be adequately prepared for college, but in a position to thrive in school academically."
- "While North Star alumni are highly educated, their annual earned income is not particularly high."

Prior Schooling, Satisfaction, and Likelihood to Enroll Again
- "Seventy-nine percent of participants reported attending public school before joining North Star, four percent attended private school, and seventeen percent homeschooled."
- North Star alumni reported being overwhelmingly satisfied with their experiences, with fifty-six percent stating they were Strongly Satisfied, forty-two percent stating they were Somewhat Satisfied, and only one participant stating they were Somewhat Dissatisfied. No one indicated Strongly Dissatisfied."
- Voting rates among North Star alumni were incredibly high, with eighty-eight percent stating they voted in a state or federal election in the past five years.
- As it is impossible to obtain a control sample, it is difficult to tell if North Star alumni have meaningfully higher self-esteem scores than the general public; however, it is clear from these results that alumni have healthy levels of self-esteem.

Alumni Statements about Equality in Relationships with Adults
- "They (North Star staff) were really calm and really respectful of the process of me struggling in front of them."

- "I felt valued as a person there (at North Star) rather than subjugated as—I don't know—some kind of inferior or something like that, which is how I felt in high school."

Alumni Statements about Sense of Agency, Freedom, and Control

- Emily wrote, "North Star alumni frequently noted gaining a sense of agency or freedom that carried with them to further educational, life, and employment pursuits."
- "I think it (my learning experience at North Star) was a lot of me studying on my own and learning that I could go on my own and learn at my own pace. Learning the philosophy of North Star, and the teachers that I had, followed me later and helped me when I was doing my own academics."
- "Just being able to direct your own future, your own activity at a young age, I realized consequences and responsibility when the risk may not be as high."
- "At college, I think I was able to really focus on academics because I knew that I didn't really have to be there. I knew I was choosing to be there. Does that make sense? And I really learned that, I learned that from Pathfinder."
- "You know, one thing I noticed, actually, was that when I was in school, the way that I presented my appearance was kind of a rebellion against school. And I would dye my hair all these crazy colors and I wore really thick black liquid eyeliner and kind of gothic clothes. And it was really interesting: as soon as I got to North Star, I don't know, the I way I presented myself changed a lot because I no longer had anything to fight against. And I just kind of began to feel comfortable. And I was still creative with my appearance but it got a lot more lighter and a lot more joyful."
- "Not one person [at North Star] ever called me to an annoyance meeting (laughs.) I think this is pretty remarkable if you want to view it through that compar-

ison, because when I was in high school I was usually either externally suspended or kicked out of class."

Alumni Statements on North Star's Impact on Future Educational Experiences

- Emily wrote, "North Star alumni frequently gained qualities of self-direction, independence, critical thinking and purpose that are forms of higher status cultural capital...North Star alumni who attended college emphasized that North Star gave them capacities that not only let them thrive in school, but also developed skills and attributes that put them ahead of their peers."

- Emily continued, "The lack of grading structure was specifically beneficial to students who experienced mental health challenges or had learning disabilities."

- Emily added, "North Star alumni who did not attend college frequently noted that North Star did not disable them from accessing this institution; instead, these alumni framed their experiences as allowing them to build their confidence in choosing not to go to college at a typical age. They also expressed that college was something they would go to when they feel it is applicable to their lives."

- "...meeting with Susannah I sort of found psychology. And I figured out that's what I wanted to do, you know, by learning what sort of reading materials I was drawn towards. So I think she really helped me figure out what it was that I wanted to do and work on."

- "I don't think I would have ever started a business if I hadn't gone to North Star. But the experience of North Star really opened up my eyes to that possibility, especially because one of the classes that I took at North Star was a business class...where the teacher would take us to local businesses and we would talk to the local business owners about what it was like to start their own business. And he really instilled a lot of ideas into us that still stay with me, insofar as how it works

and how normal people can start businesses and how to be smart about it. "
- "North Star taught me to look, to really own the work that I'm doing. And to take self-direction. And to, yeah, drive myself through the work...I have these qualities that I think North Star really helped me develop and I think that I seek employers that value those aspects in me. Because they are part of my identity."
- "I still look for jobs where I can have a lot of self-direction. Jobs that can fit a lifestyle where I can have a lot of self-direction and openness. I'm a nurse now, but...I look for jobs where I'm sort of my own guide in deciding how to do the job best."

Emily's conclusion:

"Overall, findings indicate that North Star alumni's alternative educational experience does not inhibit their access to employment or educational opportunities, nor does it negatively impact their ability to function socially as an adult. Additionally, the findings suggest that North Star alumni understand their educational experiences as having benefitted them as adults, including performance in higher education, seeking certain jobs, and building stronger self-concepts and social skills than what they would otherwise have possessed."

Emily's primary concern:

Emily reports that most of the respondents to her survey were white, and that overall North Star's alumni population is overwhelmingly white. North Star's population is not as diverse as some local public schools, and this fact raises questions.

Could North Star work for a more racially diverse population? Is the limited diversity of North Star due to its outreach efforts, its staffing history, its curriculum content, or any other messages it sends to the local community? For North Star to hold some larger role in national education reform, Emily proposes that these questions must be addressed.

Ken's Response to Emily's Capstone Research

Emily did her work with complete, unfettered access to all North Star alumni. She received guidance from professors at Warren Wilson whom I have never met. I therefore feel some genuine confirmation from her report. I remain open and interested in further examinations of our alumni data, and the people themselves, as we progress.

I share Emily's concern that North Star has had relatively few students of color as members. Based on my teaching experience in our local public schools, I think many teens of color might benefit from our approach.

I have a few potential explanations for the fact that there have been few North Star members from these communities over the years.

First, our area is predominantly white.

Second, many families of color are working as hard as they can to keep their children in school, and have limited interest in experimenting with a non-diploma granting program. I know the powerful historical efforts and risks that were involved in integrating public schools during my lifetime, and it is hard for parents to turn away from that goal.

Third, our staff has been almost exclusively white, made up of people who volunteered at North Star prior to becoming paid staff.

Fourth, we have not had a directed outreach effort specifically targeting teens and families of color, as we have not held any targeted advertising campaigns at all. We have relied on word-of-mouth, and as Emily notes, word-of-mouth tends to bring more people like those already involved.

I find it noteworthy that North Star has had many teens who come from multi-racial families, often more than twenty percent of our members. Many of these teens find the social scene at middle school and high school exclusionary or difficult to navigate.

I have every confidence that the North Star model would thrive in an urban environment or for students of color in our community. I am encouraged by the success of Catherine Gobron's program, LighthouseHolyoke, focused primarily on Puerto Rican students in Holyoke, Massachusetts. (More in Chapter 11.)

As I reflect on the students I taught back in the 1990s in Prince George's County, Maryland, I wish I could offer them my services now.

A program aimed fully at a low-income community, such as the one that I taught in (Suitland, Maryland), would need to have a different funding model than North Star. I see money to fund a program, rather than the race or class of potential students, as the major obstacle to supporting a North Star program in an urban setting.

Final thoughts

From midwives to morticians, farmers to chefs, first responders to doctors, early childhood teachers to superintendents, carpenters to realtors, ordinary workers to entrepreneurs, North Star alumni can tend to all of our needs. They are professional musicians, artists, and athletes—including a bike racer and a circus performer. Many speak other languages, and have traveled the world.

As I step back and look at the outcomes, especially at older alumni over age 30, I have to wonder: How much did North Star matter? Would these people have become who they are anyway, with more of their interests and identities developing after high school?

For most adults, high school is a distant memory, mostly socially oriented, and we credit our adult outcomes to other young-adult experiences. Perhaps North Star was little more than "a strange version of high school" for our alumni, who went on to live their lives much as they would have, had they completed school.

I have two responses to my own question, one modest and one fierce.

The modest response is this: At a minimum, North Star helped teens live more happy, interesting, and meaningful lives during their teen years. Even if North Star wasn't pivotal in their life trajectories, our members opted out of traditional school for a reason. North Star supported them to try something unique, contrary to popular culture, and sent them on their way at least as well off as if they had stayed in school. We haven't made anyone's life worse, and that's different from how I felt when I was teaching middle school.

This "Do No Harm" argument is something deeply satisfying to me, but others associated with North Star find it appallingly modest. There is a much stronger response to my question.

North Star has welcomed every interested family that has wanted to join our program. We have no admissions policy, no waiting list, no lotteries. We are not selecting members to improve our odds of positive outcomes. We are not excluding people who appear to be difficult cases. We embrace families, regardless of their ability to pay or contribute to North Star.

After the 2016 U.S. presidential election, I felt compelled to hang a poster of the Statue of Liberty in our front entry way, with the famous stanza of Emma Lazarus' poem *The New Colossus:*

"Give me your tired, your poor, your huddled masses yearning to breathe free, the wretched refuse from your teeming shore. Send these, the homeless, tempest-tossed to me. I lift my lamp beside the golden door."

In some sense, North Star has provided a refuge for students who have felt trapped in an institution, with years to go before graduation.

We have welcomed teens with severe anxiety, depression, or other mental health issues, including self-harming and suicidal ideation. We have met teens who are angry at school, their parents, and even at me, in our first meetings. Our relationships often begin with their wary fear or resistance.

Others arrive with dreams that not only fall outside of their school's curricula, but also outside of their family's vision. North Star has embraced the struggling, the resistant, the eccentric, as well as the healthy high-achiever who just wants a head start on life. Our alumni outcomes reflect our serious commitment to welcoming teens where they are in their lives when they arrive, and discovering what support they wish to receive from us.

Our staff's close relationships with current members and alumni leave us certain that we are, indeed, having a pivotal impact on the lives of our members. For our long-term members, we offer not only an immediate improvement in their lives unimaginable for them in a school program, but we also see them through the transition from North Star to young adulthood.

We are part of the process; a necessary and irreplaceable part. For our short-term members, we offer a positive respite from schooling. We pull them from an experience in which they may feel like they are drowning. We dry them off, then help them take a breath and reconsider their options. It is rare for schools to offer this option in the calm, confident, and visionary way that North Star does.

As both my report and Emily's research indicate, North Star alumni remember that they were members of our program, and they can identify certain behaviors and attitudes they retain from their time with us. The closer one is to North Star—staff, board, parent, alumni—the more one is inspired by the lives that have been changed for the better.

North Star changes lives in profound ways that rarely happen in school, and leaves lasting impressions on all of us. North Star is a pivotal life experience for many of its members, and our success merits recognition, celebration, and further investigation.

One Member's Journey

As a fitting end to this chapter, I am delighted to share a Facebook post by Lia Ashe-Simmer. At the time of this writing, Lia is 23 years old. She compiled this list mostly for her own satisfaction, and I saw it just when I was reviewing this chapter. I feel Lia captures the spirit I aim to convey, and appreciate her allowing me to include it here:

> *When I was 16, I decided not to go back to high school; which, looking back, was one of those "crossroads" people talk about. But also, I was so miserable that it wasn't much of a decision, as it was a necessity. Lately, I've been reflecting on some of the things I've done since then, and it's actually pretty crazy. I've never looked at it in linear terms, but it's fun to write it all down.*
>
> *Since I left high school at 16, I:*
>
> - *met my best friend, Isabel, at North Star*
>
> - *wrote a lot*
>
> - *took some really interesting classes/tutorials at North Star*
>
> - *took more classes at GCC*
>
> - *volunteered in a kindergarten classroom*
>
> - *learned how to downhill ski (which I will have to relearn at some point)*
>
> - *traveled solo for the first time to Heredia, Costa Rica*
>
> - *tutored at a middle school*
>
> - *transferred to Earlham College in Richmond, IN*
>
> - *met my other best friends, Lilly and Minori*
>
> - *did a study abroad in Ocotal, Nicaragua*
>
> - *went tubing and lost my 14-year-old lizard bracelet in the process. It's probably still there!*
>
> - *climbed part of a volcano with Lilly*

- *biked around an island*

- *swam in a hot spring*

- *met a memorable tour guide named Willy, and a Swede named Sven*

- *left Earlham, and returned to Nicaragua…solo, this time*

- *got TEFL (Teaching English as a Foreign Language) certified in Leon; met so many great people during the course whom I still think about a lot!*

- *rented an apartment in Leon with some amazing human beings, Anna and Jerline. It had an open roof and an amazing hammock and a garden right in the middle!*

- *volcano boarded (I got stuck halfway down)*

- *traveled to Costa Rica and Guatemala to see Isabel (and visited Honduras and El Salvador briefly, en route to Guatemala)*

- *got in a terrifying tuk-tuk accident in Guatemala. EEK!*

- *taught English at a private school near Leon (I was 19 and teaching a rowdy group of 13- to 17-year-olds…EEK, again!)*

- au-paired *briefly in Spain; stayed with two nice families and one not-so-nice one.*

- *visited England for the first time in 10 years; saw lots of family*

- *biked part of the Great Allegheny Passage with my dad*

- *worked at a YMCA summer camp*

- *worked at an after-school program*

- *worked as a caretaker for a woman with dementia*

- *got my driver's license*

- *traveled to Barbados to see Minori*

- *traveled to Bloomington, IN to see Lilly*

- *graduated from UMass Amherst*

- *wrote a creative writing thesis thingy*

- *and since July, have been working as an English teacher in Chile.*

Of course, there's a lot missing from this list, and not everything was easy. In fact, there were A LOT of hard times in there, too, a lot of confusion and sleepless nights and anxiety and just general stress. But even so, life is amazing, or, at the very least, has the potential to be amazing. And it was so satisfying to write it all down, and remember that even in the not-so-great times, I had some pretty great experiences. And there are a lot of great people in the world. So that's it. Sorry if I sound like a self-obsessed millennial.

11

Spreading the Model through Liberated Learners

When we started Pathfinder in 1996, Joshua Hornick and I had some big dreams about establishing a model program that others would emulate. "Every teen doesn't have to join Pathfinder," we said, "but there should be a Pathfinder in every community!" We imagined that our model would be simple and efficient enough that other disillusioned teachers and veteran homeschooling parents could provide an alternative to school for teens everywhere.

Alas, we soon learned that we were only half-right. Pathfinder was simple and efficient, but as such, it generated low revenue and didn't provide an easy route to a reliable salary for its staff. We were making a difference in the lives of our members, but we weren't creating a sustainable model for the staff. We had many inspirational stories, but we really did not have a model worth sharing. In fact, after seven years, as previously mentioned, Joshua left the staff and became the president of the Board of Directors.

I faced the question of whether to keep North Star going, and if so, how to evaluate my own success. I decided that North Star was fulfilling to me, and that it was making a positive impact for many teens and families. I would keep it going as long as I found it satisfying and it wasn't requiring major cash infusions from me.

I chose to release the goal of making North Star replicable for anyone. It was clear that my plate was full managing and stabilizing this single program, and that I would only make myself feel depressed if my standard for success was that North Star be replicable. In my own head, even though North Star was a non-profit organization, I developed the sense that North Star was similar to a private business (such as my father's jewelry store, or a bakery or other valued enterprise) that may or may not outlive its founders. That would be an open question, but in the meantime, the enterprise would offer a needed and valuable service to the community with the goal of becoming financially secure.

North Star celebrated its ten-year anniversary, and we felt proud of our alumni and our accomplishments. We had stories to tell about making school optional for teens. We wanted people to know that by providing a modicum of support for families feeling trapped in school, one could have a profound impact on their ability to make the life-altering choice of using homeschooling and self-directed learning.

We didn't have a solid blueprint for how to make a living doing so, but we had a method and an idea that needed to be heard. In 2007, Joshua convinced me that we should hold our first "Replication Conference" over a spring weekend. Five people attended. They were all sincerely interested in the model, and I've remained in touch with a couple of them. One of these participants was completely convinced, and committed to starting a center of his own: Joel Hammon.

It turns out that Joel, like me, grew up in Ohio and became a public school teacher. He is about ten years younger than I am, and he had followed a similar path of becoming discouraged trying to get kids to want to learn what he was required to teach them. He had a stable, well-paid job in a public school outside of Philadelphia, Pennsylvania, but he would sometimes despair and conduct late-night Internet searches for "Jobs for teachers who hate teaching in schools."

One of these dark nights, North Star popped up on his screen. Joel reports that, after reading about North Star online, "I threw my papers high in the air and did a happy dance in my room!" He had found us.

Thus began Joel's four-year planning process to start a center in his area. He spent time finding partners, cultivating community relationships, and researching homeschooling and unschooling. He wanted his center to thrive within a year or two of starting. Joel is a family man, and he needed to earn a solid salary relatively quickly. During those four years, I made a couple of trips to Princeton to meet his potential colleagues and convince them that this model was a good idea.

In 2010, Princeton Learning Cooperative opened its pilot program. Joel was still teaching in school, organizing PLC on the side, while co-founder Paul Scutt staffed the program each day. They had six members by the end of that year. In June, 2011, Joel resigned his job to become a full-time staff member at PLC.

That second fall, the membership increased to eight or nine members. Fortunately, a local newspaper published an article about PLC, and they had a sudden flood of members in February and March, 2012. Joel, Paul, and their third colleague—veteran homeschooling parent Alison Snieckus—seized on the momentum and have been thriving since that time.

I was initially surprised and thrilled at their success. They had the courage and need to charge a higher membership fee for PLC than we charged for North Star, and it was working for them. Their tweaks, innovations, and expansions of the model have been instructive to me. I found I enjoyed having peers who were facing the same problems I had been facing, and now I could observe and learn from their responses and solutions.

These innovations were not just about fees, but also about providing advisory services to teens and families, creating an interesting schedule of programs, envisioning the ideal size of the membership, and more. It was like they were holding up a mirror, and I could consider some things in a fresh way. We didn't feel the need to agree on all of these items, and the discussions were challenging and helpful.

In 2016, Joel published his book, *The Teacher Liberation Handbook: How to Leave School and Create a Place Where You and Young People Can Thrive,* aimed at inspiring other disillusioned teachers to join us in this field. In it, he recounts his experience and shares the major lessons he has learned in building a team and growing a program. Joel's insights and details about the start-up phase of creating a program are a wealth of information for those seriously interested in establishing a program in their communities.

To this point, North Star had largely been operating on its own, making decisions within the Board of Directors and the Core Staff, with no other models to follow or colleagues with whom to compare notes. I had spent time explaining to others that North Star was neither 1) a program for existing homeschoolers similar to many successful homeschooling models around the country, nor 2) an alternative private school, such as Sudbury Valley School or any other democratic/free school modeled after Summerhill.

We didn't fit into any familiar slots.

As I noted earlier in this book, North Star was not a homeschooling co-op, because we weren't targeting existing homeschoolers. Our goal was to help school-bound families opt out of school, using the homeschooling law as the legal mechanism to do so. We welcomed existing homeschoolers who wanted to join our program, but we could see that we were more expensive and offered more services than what most of these families would want. We also believed in allowing members to come to North Star to socialize or sit quietly without attending classes, a practice considered odd to many independent homeschooling families.

North Star was not a private school, either. We had some philosophy in common with some of the most "open" schools, but those schools expected students to attend five days per week through age 18, and to earn a high school diploma for this effort. North Star had no attendance requirement, nor any diploma to offer its members.

We weren't providing the same basic services as a private school, even when we held in common some principles about self-directed learning.

Joel, Paul, and Alison, along with their team at PLC, were the first people to grasp our model and choose to emulate it. There is a humorous TED Talk by Derek Sivers that offers a telling insight into what Joel and PLC represent to me and to North Star. The TED Talk is called, "How to Start a Movement."

In three minutes, Derek describes the important role of a "First Follower," turning a "Lone Nut" into a "Leader of a Movement." I encourage you to stop reading and watch it right now.

In October, 2017, Joel gave his own TEDx Talk, describing his transition from discouraged public school history teacher to the co-founder of Princeton Learning Cooperative, and now a mentor for others interested in starting their own centers.

While Joel was spending four years organizing PLC from 2007-2010, I was attending the annual Alternative Education Resource Organization's annual conference, then being held in upstate New York.

I would offer two workshops: a teen panel of North Star members and alumni sharing their experiences; and another, entitled "Start Right Now!" that encouraged conference attendees to support teens in opting out of school. I met a range of fascinating people, who were leaders and doers in the field of alternative education, and I continue to attend this annual conference most years.

In 2011, AERO moved its conference to the West Coast, and I wasn't going to be able to make that trip. We (North Star and PLC) decided to offer our own conference that summer, doing the workshops we would have conducted at the AERO Conference, plus a bit more.

We had several attendees, and the effort led to two start-up groups: Compass in Ottawa, Quebec and Beacon in New Haven, Connecticut. We continued holding a summer conference, and in the subsequent years supported the creation of Deep Root Center in Canton, New York, and Bay State Learning Center in Dedham, Massachusetts.

Over the next few years, we had many other attendees (approximately 8 groups and 25 or more participants each year) and we helped a few other centers get started, but we were still scaring people off from starting a program because we did not have a solid financial model to present to them. We were (and still are) proposing that a combination of membership fees and fundraising is needed to cover overhead and salaries.

We had no access to public money, nor any major foundations or grants that were ready to support others in emulating our model. We had a unique educational approach that was attractive to many, but it wasn't compelling to people already earning a decent living as public school teachers. The model was too uncertain.

Despite these concerns, the inquiries and consulting continued. In 2013, we decided it was time to establish a separate organization for this work, rather than have the consulting be part of North Star's organization. We established Liberated Learners, Inc., a network of the centers based on the North Star model. North Star and Princeton Learning Cooperative and the others already established were equal founding members, and Liberated Learners became the organization to disseminate information, consult with others, and perhaps attract resources that might be shared among them.

Rather than franchising the North Star model, we are using Liberated Learners as something of an "open-source" platform among the member centers, to report our experiences and compare our experiments with how to offer our services. We are all dedicated to supporting teens and families to use self-directed learning as an alternative to school, but we are each free to do so according to our visions, personalities, and local communities.

Liberated Learners has an ongoing email group, in which all members can exchange questions and ideas. We have an annual conference each June. We exchange various documents, blog posts, and other materials, including an online portfolio system designed specifically for our centers. We visit each other's centers. We imagine the possibilities of sharing some administrative staff and applying for grants together.

I prefer this sort of mutual support, rather than some version of franchising North Star and then supervising each center's implementation of the model. Currently, the non-negotiable elements of a Liberated Learners program are as follows (taken from the Liberated Learners website):

Liberated Learners centers embrace the following principles:

- Centers adopt a mission of helping children and teens leave school, using homeschooling law to improve their lives and learning, and of helping existing homeschoolers sustain or improve their use of this approach.
- All center activities and attendance are strictly optional.
- Centers are not accredited "schools" (nor should they use school, academy or other such synonyms in their names), and therefore do not offer grades, credits, or diplomas, or require testing of their members.
- Centers maintain a physical space, open on a regular schedule, where members, staff, and volunteers participate in various group and individual endeavors, such as classes, workshops, advising, tutorials, and meetings with families.

We have seen that this network is not sufficient to help everybody grow through the first year of starting a center. We have seen several programs open, then shut down when the enrollment and revenue are insufficient, including efforts in Portland, Oregon, Collinsville, Connecticut, and Leominster, Massachusetts. These experiences have led us to revise our consulting procedures.

As of 2017-2018, we begin the consulting process with a one-time, no-charge phone call, to hear people's visions and experiences and to answer their first questions. If they want to proceed, we offer a webinar for a small fee, in which Joel and I provide more details about the model, and what we believe is needed to get a program through the initial stages to some sort of stability.

When people find this information inspiring, we have a Starter package, which involves a series of six conversations to work through our extensive planning document. At the end of this Starter process, both the Starter group and the Liberated Learners Board must agree to proceed, with some confidence that this program is ready to get started. At that point, the new program officially joins Liberated Learners.

At our 2018 Liberated Learners Conference, we discussed more ways that our centers might interact and support one another, particularly in the fields of interactive programming, student exchanges, grant writing, and network-wide purchasing of services and resources.

Our reflections on this refined process in 2017 are positive: We have seen a solid launch of The Embark Center in Leesburg, Virginia, and the opening in early 2018 of BigFish Learning Community in Dover, New Hampshire.

In November, 2016, we invited Grace Llewellyn, author of the inspirational and previously mentioned *Teenage Liberation Handbook* (which I have given out to nearly every inquiring family over the years), to speak at North Star's twentieth-year celebration. Grace joined us and left so inspired by our community, that she decided she should start her own program in Eugene, Oregon. She planned The Hive during 2017. We have now inspired the person who inspired us to start North Star! That counts as a lifetime accomplishment for me.

As of Fall, 2018, it appears the next center joining Liberated Learners sometime in 2018-2019 will be Abot Tala in Manila, The Philippines. This group hosted me for a visit in July, 2018, which I summarized in a blog post on our Liberated Learners site. I am encouraged that this project is proceeding carefully and optimistically.

Several other groups that have participated in the Starter process have chosen to delay opening a program and becoming a member of Liberated Learners, mainly due to a lack of capital. Our efforts to support the founding team in building a Board of Directors and amassing the funds necessary to get through the first stage of launching a program only go so far. Liberated Learners does not provide start-up funding, so as in any business start-up, working capital is a major obstacle for people wishing to create a program.

As I wrote in Chapter 8: In 2015, Catherine Gobron left North Star to start a new program called LightHouse: Personalized Education for Teens, with former North Star Board Member Josiah Litant. They were both engaged with the community of Holyoke, a small city with a public school system comprised of mostly Puerto Rican students.

The system was faring so poorly that it was taken over by the Massachusetts Board of Education in 2015. The LightHouse team wanted to bring the North Star model to Holyoke, and provide an exciting and effective alternative to these students and families who truly needed some spark and improvement. Now in its fourth year, LightHouse is operating at capacity, and is indeed making a difference for its members.

LightHouse has chosen to operate somewhat differently than North Star, in terms of its structure. Catherine and Josiah are developing positive relationships with the Holyoke Public Schools. As they nurture this relationship and other aspects of the Lighthouse program that might conflict with Liberated Learners philosophy, as of 2018, they have chosen to withdraw from Liberated Learners.

We remain friends and allies, and we in Liberated Learners are hopeful that LightHouse's relationship with the Holyoke Public Schools might lead to some breakthroughs for other centers in our network. Their work is also a model for those wondering whether this approach of self-directed learning can work in an urban setting.

There are two elements of LightHouse's start-up phase that are particularly noteworthy. First, Catherine and Josiah fully committed themselves to a process of meeting people in Holyoke and asking them what might be useful for teens in that city. They had a model to bring, but they also listened, requested opinions, and solicited further referrals of more people to meet. They spent a year doing hundreds of face-to-face conversations in Holyoke, to build relationships and introduce themselves and the model to people working with youth and families in the community. The time and effort they spent was gargantuan, and it has paid off for them.

Second, they had the ability to attract a pool of donors, including one "angel donor," who made it possible for LightHouse to construct a beautiful facility in a repurposed old mill building, and who also provided important dollars towards the annual operating costs for the first several years. This preliminary funding was essential to their start-up phase. Their success in this realm extends the range of what we see as possible strategies for starting a center.

In late 2017, we were contacted by a number of people who are already working with teens using a home-schooling or self-directed learning framework, including people in California, New Hampshire, North Carolina, Ontario, and Brooklyn, New York. I average about one introductory phone call per week, with people curious to learn about North Star and Liberated Learners. We believe our consulting process will lead to either solid start-ups or wise delays for the people interested in using this model.

We also receive inquiries from around the world. Just in 2017-2018 alone, I spoke with people from Vietnam, Guatemala, Russia, Lithuania, Denmark, South Africa, Australia, England, Italy, The Bahamas, Belgium, India, and Canada. These conversations show me that the frustration with schooling is with the system, not one local town or state's way of implementing school. People feel trapped, delayed, and oppressed by the long and sometimes meaningless road of schooling all around the world, and there is a quest for alternatives and innovation everywhere.

In many of these countries (including Russia, to my surprise), homeschooling is a legal option for families, and the idea of establishing a center to spread this approach for teens feeling trapped in school is completely plausible. In some countries, homeschooling is not legal, and the options for teens who do not complete school are bleak.

In my remarks at North Star's annual Celebration of Self-Directed Learning in November, 2017, I related how these conversations make me feel somewhat patriotic about the United States. I have learned that U.S. culture is particularly open to teens who do not thrive in school. We have many ways for young adults (or older adults) to attend college, enter professions, and improve their lives even if they did poorly in, or did not graduate from, high school. I find the flexibility and openness of our culture inspiring, and I'm delighted that the North Star model brings some of this openness to teenagers.

As I believe I've made abundantly clear, I welcome the challenge of making North Star sustainable, and I want to coach others to use this model, but I have no desire to be directly in charge of more centers.

I deeply value my relationships with Joel Hammon and Alison Snieckus, staff members of the Princeton Learning Cooperative, who for the past ten years have pushed, challenged, and led me to consider the model from many angles. They are the instigators and Board members for Liberated Learners. I appreciate the innovation and camaraderie of all the members of Liberated Learners. I imagine that I will shift more of my working time from North Star to Liberated Learners in the coming decade or two.

I am acutely aware of the limits of this model. I am thrilled that at least a handful of Liberated Learners centers are thriving, showing that the model is tenable. Some teams are succeeding in building a program based on membership fees and fundraising to cover their costs and pay reasonable salaries. I also see how difficult and tenuous this process is without a solid source of public money, foundation support, or other financial security.

For now, just as I have been coaching one family at a time to leave school and embark on self-directed learning with North Star, we at Liberated Learners are coaching one team at a time to start up and build their own programs. This may not be a comprehensive solution, but it is satisfying for the moment, while I observe the changes and developments in education reform more broadly. The widespread and growing interest in our model suggests we are offering an original and inspiring solution to the ingrained problems of compulsory schooling.

12

Modern Education Reform: Where Does North Star Fit In?

Where does North Star fit into the current landscape and future of education reform? In the first part of the twenty-first century, United States education reform is a complicated landscape. Public schools face an era demanding accountability and test results. Some reformers, including former President Barack Obama, are calling for longer school days and year-round schooling.

Many reformers are pushing for families to have more choices over which schools their children attend. This movement for choice includes proponents of charter schools, School Choice, vouchers for private schools, and new options such as Education Savings Accounts.

Homeschooling sits on the fringe of these reforms, offering some families the escape valve of "none of the above, thank you." This last chapter will explore North Star's relationship to each of these options, and consider some visions for how things might evolve in the coming years and decades.

My personal life has encompassed many of these options. My wife and I (and all of our siblings and cousins) grew up attending public schools. Our positive experiences led us to become public school teachers. When our children were young, my wife and I chose to use an alternative private school for their elementary school years. This decision raised questions among our parents due to the private school status, not the alternative approach.

Our son, Sam, then enrolled in our local public school for grades 7-12, where he had a very positive experience. (He proceeded directly on to college, and graduated in four years.) Our daughter, Claudia, stayed in a private school through eighth grade, and then we utilized School Choice to enroll her in a neighboring town's public high school.

With that school's approval, she participated in a semester program with Kroka Expeditions in eleventh grade. She used Dual Enrollment at Greenfield Community College for twelfth grade. She took a year off after high school, then started full-time college with enough credits to have sophomore standing, utilizing the ideas of North Star without ever joining the program. (See the Epilogue for Sam's and Claudia's versions of these stories.)

Both of our children received traditional high school diplomas. We considered some of the well-respected local charter schools for each of our children, but did not use them. Incidentally, while I've been running North Star, my wife has worked at a local history museum, training teachers; taught at a charter school for one year; and now teaches adult immigrants English, with a local non-profit organization. Based on my family's experiences, I have some direct understanding of these schooling options and what is required for families to use them.

At North Star, I have welcomed teens coming from all of these options as well. The majority of members have come from traditional public schools, but many have come from charter schools, private schools, or independent homeschooling experiences. I have a fairly clear picture of how families consider the pros and cons of each of these options, as well as what the social costs and benefits related to making these options more available might be.

Choice as a Concept in Education

Before I consider each of the current education reform models, I want to clarify my support for offering choices to teens and families about learning and schooling. My position is that I'd like to see all students offered as much choice as possible. For me, choice is about much more than which school to attend, or which courses to take at a compulsory school. For me, choice is about the full spectrum of what to learn, how to learn it, with whom to learn it, and the ability to decide when one has learned a sufficient amount.

In my experience, forcing people to learn things does not result in long-term, internalized learning, and I believe that external requirements diminish the sense of joy, initiative, and ownership people may feel about their learning (see Alfie Kohn, Peter Gray).

I believe that offering choice works for two complementary reasons: First, when people have choice, they have to honor the opportunity and effort involved in choosing the activity. Asking for materials, tutors, or classes demands a reasonable commitment from the student to justify the energy and costs necessary in identifying and utilizing these resources.

Naturally, students who choose a class, a program within a school, or a different school altogether must recognize that they are receiving something that is not automatically theirs. If they value the option and want to continue with this learning process, they must honor the situation for everyone making it possible. This situation normally leads to more engaged behavior and better learning outcomes.

The complementary reason that choice works involves considering the situation from the perspective of the teacher or the school. This is as freeing for the teacher or the school as it is for the student.

When students choose a course, a program, or a school, and then act as if they don't want to be there, the school has some recourse. A teacher might say, "It seems you don't really want to be here. If that's the case, I'd be happy to work with you in some other way, but please feel free to leave." A school can say, "We have a long waiting list. If you don't want to be here, we'd like to give your slot to someone who does." The process of choice allows instructors and schools the freedom to decline uninterested or disruptive students.

Choice works both ways: Students should not be forced to learn things that don't interest them, and teachers should not be forced to teach students who are not interested in what they have to offer.

I recognize that the idea of asking uninterested students to leave a classroom or a school goes against all sentiment, training, and obligation of public schooling. I know that previous racist policies and behaviors by those in power make exclusion a dangerous and suspect idea.

As a public school teacher, removing students from my classroom was an act of last resort. It was an admission of failure, of weakness, of an inability to manage my classroom. It also violated the school's message that "No child is unteachable," or "No child is unwelcome," in our community.

I value those sentiments. I have dedicated my North Star career to creating a welcoming and non-judgmental environment that conveys the message that every person has interests and talents. However, I no longer apply this moral stance to a coercive process. I see compulsory schooling as the first violation of a student's choice, and therefore all solutions must include an option about whether and how frequently to attend school at all.

My intention is not to violate students' rights to an education, but rather to define an additional right that Blake Boles and others refer to as "educational consent." Blake is a leading author, speaker, and podcaster in the field of self-directed learning (blakeboles.com).

His three books include *The Art of Self-Directed Learning, College Without High School,* and *Better Than College.* He defines his version of this idea in a 2018 YouTube video, "To Fix Education, Make it Consensual." (https://www.youtube.com/watch?v=g1Xlst7O4TM)

Current Public School Reform

As I mentioned above, both of my children attended public high schools and earned diplomas. Each of them

had some outstanding teachers, and each had very positive experiences with sports and clubs. The schools they
attended are the central common experience for youth in
their communities, and their day-to-day routines were reasonably familiar to what I remember of my own experience
at Shaker Heights High School.

The state testing, which did not exist in its current
form in my teen years, does occupy a lot of time and
attention. Overall, I think there is little desire among my
children or their peers for longer school days or longer
school years. School is pretty stable and predictable, and
the vast majority of students use it as best they can.

I found my children's graduation ceremonies to be
happy community events, but they left me with one primary
critique. The graduation speakers presented school as if
it were a long journey with only one acceptable outcome:
graduation. They congratulated students for making it to
that point, as if school were a divided highway with one exit
tollbooth, through which the students were now passing.

In this book, I have tried to show that learning is, in
fact, a rather ordinary road with many turnoffs, and that
people may choose to travel successfully in many other
ways and in different directions.

I recognize that public schools remain the primary
option for most children in the United States, and that
many good people are offering quality opportunities within
them. At this point, I do not see public schools embracing
the North Star model. Schools don't seem to be ready to
accept part-time attendance, student selection of courses,
and a GED or other exam as a valid method for an early
completion of schooling.

However, as of Spring, 2018, I have learned about
two new public schools that may prove me wrong:,
UnSchool, part of the San Juan Unified School District
in Fair Oaks, California, and Powderhouse Studios in
Somerville, Massachusetts.

UnSchool completed its first academic year in 2017-
2018, with approximately 80 students attending ninth and

tenth grades. The principal, Gabriel Cooper, had been working in the Sacramento Public Schools for eighteen years, when the superintendent approached him to start a school that might appeal to some of the students and families choosing charter schools and homeschooling.

While students are expected to attend UnSchool on a daily basis, there is an extraordinary amount of flexibility for how students can spend their time in the building. Also, UnSchool supports students spending time off-campus doing various sorts of projects or work. The advisory system, where students meet with staff on a daily basis, is a central feature of the program.

UnSchool has been warmly received by the Sacramento community, and Gabe is optimistic about where things stand at this time. There will be some issues to work out as students and staff assign credits to various projects as students move towards graduation, but the school system's commitment to the program should allow for a positive process and outcome.

I completed my conversation with Gabe feeling somewhat stunned. He had gone in a different direction than I had chosen, sticking with public school administration for fifteen years, in contrast to my choice to leave the system. Now he has a visionary and risk-taking superintendent backing him to create a self-directed learning model as a public school in Sacramento. I had foreclosed this possibility as "impossible," and now I'm learning that I was, happily, wrong!

Gabe, in evidence of his good nature, told me that we are now more than two decades after my own decision-making, and that to some extent, the success of North Star and other self-directed learning models over the past two decades have contributed to the superintendent seeing UnSchool as a worthy experiment. I look forward to following the progress of UnSchool over its next several years of growth.

Powderhouse Studios has been in the planning stages for four years, and plans to open in Fall, 2019. In this case, the mayor of Somerville, Massachusetts approached Alec

Resnick and others, who had started a small science education non-profit called Sprout & Co.

Sprout & Co. was designing and exploring tools, materials, and programs focused on making science and investigation more cultural activities than academics, through projects designed by youth. Sprout's team drew their inspiration from people such as John Holt, Ivan Illich, and Seymour Papert. With the mayor's backing, they began expanding their vision into a full-fledged Innovation School, a program of former Governor Deval Patrick that created opportunities for cities to create in-district and autonomous schools.

Powderhouse envisions a project-oriented school, where students will approach their learning much as adults approach their professional work. The website says that "Powderhouse is for students who will benefit from working in a smaller, more intimate community than a traditional high school, or spending a lot more time developing deep, hands-on projects of their own design."

The school will be open 220 days per year, and students will self-select how to complete the required amount of days and hours. In order to graduate, students will be required to pass the required state testing (tenth grade MCAS), as well as document completion of Common Core Math and English expectations. They will also have to define some next activity relating to college, training, or work that they intend to pursue.

Powderhouse states on its website that replacing a standard school curriculum with individual projects for each student may raise a lot of questions, "But overall, something which ties together a lot of our answers is flexibility and individualized support." I certainly like the sound of this vision, and I look forward to visiting Powderhouse Studios when the school opens.

Again, I had deemed the creation of this sort of public school within a larger public system to be impossible. The fact that the mayor and others in Somerville sought out a team to create a school based on a self-directed learning model surprises me, and also fills me with hope and joy.

For now, Alec shared that setting up Powderhouse within the Somerville Public Schools has required several years of what he describes as "bureaucratic and legal bushwhacking." I admire his team's endurance, patience, and vision.

Both Unschool and Powderhouse Studios are using the language of self-directed learning to help students design their own programs. I will be interested to see how these schools are affected by state testing requirements, and just what the reality becomes for any students at these schools who resist doing all of the core curriculum expectations. I am also curious to see what will happen if many students at these schools choose to withdraw and obtain a GED instead of staying through twelfth grade graduation.

Regardless of how these questions play out, these schools will be pioneers for pushing the boundaries of what may be possible within public schools, and provide me with more optimism than I have had for many years. I hope that in the coming years, many more public school systems will generate experiments involving self-directed learning.

School Choice and Charter Schools

School Choice and Charter Schools are two reforms that allow families to utilize public schools other than the school assigned to their residential address. School Choice, at least in Massachusetts, is a program through which families in one town may apply to attend a public school in a neighboring town.

Each school district determines whether it has any School Choice openings to offer to families in nearby towns. The school district must conduct a lottery if it has more School Choice applicants than slots. School Choice families do not pay any tuition for this opportunity; sending districts pay $5,000 per student to the receiving district. School Choice families must provide their own transportation. Thus, School Choice is an option for a child to change public schools at no personal cost.

Here in Massachusetts, Charter Schools are public

schools supervised by the State Board of Education, rather than a local school committee. Charter school groups apply to the State for permission to start a school, defining both a particular educational focus and a geographic area from which they will admit students. Most approved charter schools receive more applicants than they can admit, and they must use a lottery to determine who is accepted.

As is the case with School Choice, families utilizing charter schools do not pay any tuition for this opportunity; sending districts send approximately $5,000 per student to the charter school. As with School Choice, families utilizing charter schools must provide their own transportation. As public schools, charter schools must have a state-approved curriculum and implement state testing. Many people view charter schools as a way for some public families to obtain an almost private school-like environment for their children at no personal cost.

I know many teens and families who have used School Choice and charter schools with great satisfaction, including my own family, North Star's Co-Founder Joshua Hornick, and other North Star Staff Members. The families arrange carpools and find themselves having an option for one or more of their children that they prefer to their district public school.

I have two concerns with implementation of these options, and one more profound reason that I choose not to pursue these options in my professional life. My first concern is that the funding system pulls money from the district public school, such as the high school my son attended. His high school loses more students than they gain through School Choice, and they also lose many students to local charter schools. This loss, at approximately $5,000 per student, adds up to a significant budget problem for his school.

Proponents of School Choice and charter schools contend that this school should respond to competition by improving itself so that local families do not find other options more appealing. I find that argument disingenuous, to put it mildly. It is hard for a small-town local high school to compete with a neighboring public school that is larger, more affluent, and has a history of sending more graduates to elite colleges. A small high school simply cannot offer the range of electives and sports that a larger school can provide.

Also, there will always be a set of students and families who will prefer a small, cozy, charter school environment to the larger, standard public school environment. These are not level playing fields. This awareness did not stop my family from utilizing School Choice for my daughter, but we understood that we were hurting our town's public school to send her to the larger public school out of town.

A second concern I have about both of these options is that they are restricted to families who can arrange transportation. I am aware that many families make sacrifices to arrange these rides and that this problem can be resolved with some community effort. Nevertheless, many families cannot make these arrangements, and both School Choice and charter schools are options that are exclusive (as is North Star) when no public transportation is available.

These objections are fixable concerns. If the state legislature took action to protect local public schools from the financial impact of School Choice and charter schools, and if some school-supported transportation systems were established, I'd have little hesitation in supporting these options.

To complicate matters, many charter schools are run by for-profit companies, and many have missions aligned with helping low-income students improve their test scores or otherwise promote a style of learning with which I disagree. Some charter schools have been poorly run schemes to enrich their shareholders, seeing students as commodities to be recruited and retained for the funds they bring with them.

Most charter schools do not have teacher unions, and the charter school movement's motives are challenged by traditional public school proponents as being part of a wider vision to de-fund traditional public schools and disempower teacher unions. I find my personal inclinations divided: I support choice and respect the local charter schools in my area, while I also retain some doubts about the overall mission and direction of the national charter school movement.

Regardless of these political and economic issues, my deeper professional concern is that neither School Choice nor charter schools are different enough from traditional public school to address the needs I have presented in this book. North Star has welcomed many members who have used either School Choice or a charter school (or both) and discovered that it is the system of schooling—not the individual institution—that is the source of their problems.

School, as an institution, requires 6 hours of daily attendance, 180 days per year, for twelve years. It has a state-approved curriculum and demands that students sit for state testing. The teens I meet need an alternative to this type of schooling, not another school.

Vouchers

Educational vouchers provide money to families to attend a private school of their choice. According to Education Week, as of January, 2017, thirty states and the District of Columbia have voucher systems or some closely related version of private school choice.

In most systems, vouchers are available to families who meet various criteria, such as having a student with special needs, living in communities with "failing" public schools, or having a particularly low income. Some vouchers have provisions for military families, and some require that students be attending public schools prior to receiving a voucher for a private school. The amount of these vouchers ranges from $4,500 per year to more than $12,000 per year, and is frequently some percentage of a state's per-pupil education funding allocation.

Voucher proponents contend that poor families trapped in failing public school districts should not have to wait for new charter schools to be approved and created, or com-

pete in a lottery for a handful of school choice slots in neighboring districts. They want to offer financial support for these
families to utilize private schools in their communities.

In the United States, approximately eighty-five
percent of private schools are religious schools, but
the United States Supreme Court has ruled that providing parents public money to spend at private religious
schools is permissible.

As of this writing, one of the leading voucher systems in the United States comes from current Vice
President Mike Pence's home state of Indiana, where he
championed vouchers as governor. Indiana has eased the
qualifying criteria, and according to a Washington Post
review of this system, currently more than 32,000 families
receive vouchers to pay for private school, many of whom
were already enrolled at private schools before receiving
these vouchers.

There is a contentious political debate over vouchers,
and I don't want to re-argue each side here. I find myself
uncomfortable with vouchers, despite my inclinations to
want to see all families have some choices about how to
educate their children.

In my community, most private schools are very
expensive, and I don't see a public benefit to transfer-
ring money from the public system through a handful of
families to these exclusive private institutions. Despite the
Supreme Court's judgment, I am not comfortable with seeing my taxes fund religious institutions that may directly
teach content disparaging my family's religion. Vouchers
are a problematic shift of resources to established private
schools and religious institutions, in my view.

Philosophically, I don't believe parents are entitled to
control the per-pupil portion of the public school's expendi-
tures when they choose to use private school. In the United
States, taxpayers cannot demand refunds or coupons for
every publicly-funded service they do not use.

For example, if I choose not to use the public library
or public parks, I cannot expect a coupon for my portion

of these expenses to be used at private bookstores or other recreational facilities. Further, taxpayers who do not have children are not entitled to any tax relief, even though they do not and may never utilize public schools. I may selfishly wish that every family approaching North Star came with their per-pupil spending allotment in hand as a voucher, but I have yet to conclude that vouchers are good public policy.

Also, repeating myself from the previous section about School Choice and charter schools, I am not interested in a public policy that mostly expands the options for families to choose a private school for their children. Providing vouchers for private schools does not address my vision that school is optional, and that what students and families need is support to consider an alternative to a school-centered model.

Education Savings Accounts

Some homeschoolers and legislators agree with my position that families need an alternative to school, and are many steps ahead of me. One idea they are now championing is Education Savings Accounts. In this approach, approved homeschooling families with incomes under certain limits receive money they can spend on approved educational activities and materials. The amounts of these ESAs may range from a few hundred to a few thousand dollars per student, per year.

A new program in New Hampshire proposes a $3,600 per student annual allocation for parents to spend on approved educational expenses. Arizona and Nevada have passed legislation in this direction, but the programs face challenges in state courts or legislative funding processes. In California, there are some "homeschooling charter schools" that operate in a similar way. Homeschooling families enroll in a charter school that receives the per-pupil state funds, oversees the families' homeschooling progress, and approves family-directed spending of up to $2,500 per student on educational expenses.

At first blush, ESAs would be great for North Star. If

every family, especially low-income families, arrived with an ESA valued at $1,000-$5,000, we would solve most of North Star's budget problems.

However, the situation is fraught with problems. First, would North Star membership fees qualify as an "approved educational expense?" If not, could North Star redefine some of its tutoring services or classes in a way that would qualify? My guess is that any problems about qualifying could be addressed with some relatively minor tweaks, and that families would be able to use ESAs to pay North Star.

Second, state funding comes with some expectations of accountability and reporting. Many libertarian and conservative homeschoolers oppose ESAs because they see the trade-off of money for reporting to be a bad precedent for the homeschooling community.

In his movie, *Class Dismissed*, filmmaker Jeremy Stuart depicts one family's stressful experience with a "homeschooling charter school supervisor," and in the end, the family chooses to forgo the offer. Others, including the Home School Legal Defense Association, oppose ESAs because they oppose any public taxation for education.

Third, as with funding for charter schools and School Choice, I would want ESAs to be funded in a way that does not harm local public schools.

Summary

The current education reform ideas I have discussed are all highly divisive. Locally, families that utilize School Choice and charter schools are in frequent debate with the vast majority of families using traditional public schools, because of the funding system. For now, neither homeschoolers nor private school families in Massachusetts receive any public money, and these groups do not fuel the same conflict that pulling money out of the local public school system does.

North Star's mission of offering an alternative to school while receiving no public funds leaves us on the outside of this very active conflict.

The Future of North Star and Liberated Learners

What are the implications of these twenty-first century education reforms for North Star and Liberated Learners? The sentiment of "choice" certainly works in North Star's favor. Many people agree that students should not feel trapped in one school. Homeschooling has grown from less than one percent to more than three and four-tenths percent of the student population during the past few decades. I encounter a lot of interest and moral support for North Star's approach.

At the same time, the limits on our model are blatantly obvious. The major limit is financial, as previously discussed. This situation creates a major constraint on creating programs that support people to use homeschooling and self-directed learning. Programs need staff salaries and overhead that are difficult or downright impossible to fund through membership fees and fundraising in many communities.

A minor limit to the growth of programs such as North Star is public perception and fear of our approach. North Star's trust for teens may never become the dominant educational philosophy of the United States, but people are open to questioning a one-size-fits-all model. As the success of this generation's homeschoolers and self-directed learners spreads into the adult community, the points of support will grow rapidly. Based on these observations, I have developed a few possible visions for the future:

A. Continuation of the Current Process

For the foreseeable future, I will continue running North Star, helping one family at a time to utilize self-directed learning, with the goal of leaving the organization with a secure financial future. This goal likely means fundraising for an endowment of $1 million to $5 million, given my current doubts about any other solution. I will also continue consulting with others through Liberated Learners to create centers modeled on North Star, throughout the

United States and around the world. Each group will have to solve the funding problem in its own way. Liberated Learners holds a vision for a center in every community, and with some luck, we will support entrepreneurial and visionary teams to join us in this enterprise.

While I have long considered major funding to establish an endowment for North Star to be something of a pipe dream, my understanding of what may be possible was dramatically challenged by my visit to Workspace Education in March, 2018.

Workspace is a homeschooling center founded in 2016, through the vision and investment of a homeschooling community in Bethel, Connecticut. The funding primarily comes from one successful professional businessperson who has committed $4 million for Workspace, to purchase and renovate the 32,000-square-foot former Cannondale Bicycle headquarters and factory. The building has first-class resources, including a theater, a woodshop, a makerspace, a conference room, a gym, a cafeteria, and many well-organized classrooms and meeting spaces. It is also a welcoming and respectful learning community where children love spending their days.

Workspace is currently designed for homeschooling families, as it requires parental presence in the building for youth under age sixteen, but they are considering additions and changes to their model as they grow. The vision and generosity behind the establishment of Workspace exceeds whatever dreams I have allowed myself to consider to this point, and I'm now revisiting my own ideas for North Star.

I imagine that putting North Star on permanent solid financial ground will require an endowment of $1-5 million. Perhaps the effort to generate such a fund will become a central project of the next several years, partly thanks to Workspace's demonstration of what is possible.

B. Public Funding for Liberated Learners Centers

Even though I don't imagine schools creating alternative programs such as North Star, there are examples of public schools paying for an occasional student's tuition at North Star. These cases have been for teens with learning differences, usually labeled Special Needs, who have exhausted the public school's options for individual services.

When the school is faced with an out-of-district placement that can cost more than $100,000 annually, it can be in the school's interest to come up with a personalized plan that satisfies the family. On occasion, the public school's full payment of a North Star membership has been part of such a deal. One might think this is a good idea that could happen regularly, and that in other difficult cases, a local school system might offer to pay for a North Star membership as a reasonable solution.

One problem with this concept is that, as far as I understand it, schools can only pay for accredited programs out of district. I wonder if a creative public school team might be able to offer a handful of students this alternative each year, in a way that benefits everyone.

A current example of public schools paying for membership at a self-directed learning program is with LighthouseHolyoke. In that case, the city's public schools have been taken over by the state, due in part to the high dropout rate. The public schools have designated Lighthouse as an appropriate educational program, and by paying the membership fee for a handful of students, they are able to count these youth as enrolled students still engaged with education, rather than as dropouts. This experiment also seems to be good for everyone involved.

One problem with receiving public school payments has been the reality that in exchange for receiving these funds, we have had to provide attendance records and descriptions of classes and tutorials that these students have completed. This demand is not onerous, but it is outside of the normal way we do things. North Star doesn't count "attendance" at North Star or participation in our classes as more important or meaningful than engagement in other community activities.

I understand that schools want to pay for structured learning activities, and I find myself worried about whether I can always be direct about the teens' choices at North Star. I am curious to see how the reporting process works out for Lighthouse and the Holyoke Public Schools.

What happens if a student stops attending regularly, or chooses to do mostly music, or spends time writing but avoids mathematics? These questions need to be sorted out in an honest and mutually satisfactory way among the centers, the public schools, and the families involved.

Even if the public schools discover that paying for a handful of students at a center works well, I wonder what criteria and limits would be applied to such a program. They might be willing to send at-risk students on the verge of dropping out, or hard-to-serve Special Needs students, or resistant students who mostly cause trouble when they attend school. Will they also be open to sending the straight-A, non-conformist music student? The entrepreneur who wants to build a business? The scientist who wants to get a head start on a career?

It has been hard for me to imagine a publicly-funded program expanding with the sort of openness that I would want it to have. I am delighted to report that my limited imagination has been exceeded by what I have recently been told about Michigan's Homeschool Partnership programs.

Cindy Fadel, one of the founders and organizers of Partnerships has been explaining to me that these partnerships between public schools, homeschoolers, and community providers are offering a sophisticated range of options for families across the state. She estimates that there may be approximately twenty partnerships with perhaps 10,000 students participating in classes and activities.

The partnerships offer courses at no charge in public school facilities, and the community is taught by certified teachers (or community experts associated with a certified teacher) for elective credits, grades K-12. These courses include elective academics, fine arts, physical education, and much more.

In some cases, participants can even enroll in community college courses, either through dual enrollment or the Early College Program, through their partnerships. In exchange, local school districts receive pro-rated state reimbursement funds based on the number of courses students choose.

The Partnerships began in 2008, as a means for some homeschoolers to access resources and opportunities through their public schools, and a few risk-taking superintendents and legislators cautiously experimented with the idea. The concept has grown substantially in the homeschooling-friendly state of Michigan, and has been part of the increasing number of families who choose and sustain a homeschooling approach.

Cindy reports that in many partnerships, they are welcoming a new type of family from those that choose homeschooling for philosophical reasons.

"We are getting parents who say, 'We could never do homeschooling,' but with the partnership and some virtual classes, they can opt out of school, knowing they can even get a public school diploma down the line if they choose that goal."

Cindy continued that while the Partnerships may have begun as a way to pull homeschoolers into the public school community, "Now, the school parents and students see us having so much fun, flexibility, and early-college success, that we have been called an impetus for change in public education in Michigan."

I told Cindy that listening to her describe the Michigan Partnerships feels like an anthropology report, as in, "They do it differently in Michigan than in Massachusetts." I don't know how many other states may be conducting their own experiments, but the understanding that public schools and homeschoolers are working together in Michigan with positive results encourages me to re-open my imagination.

C. Private Funding for Liberated Learners Centers

Could a private donor, organization, or business support the creation of a Liberated Learners center in every community? Perhaps a wildly successful entrepreneur who hated school wants to make this alternative available to every family? Sal Khan, Bill Gates, and Oprah: I am available!

Maybe a national chain business with stores in every community has a Board of Directors that believes in the mission of Liberated Learners, and announces they will create a center in every community where they have a store?

Target, Wal-Mart, Home Depot: Perhaps some of your own employees did not thrive in school, and needed an alternative such as North Star? Or perhaps your employees' children are feeling constrained in school, but the families do not earn enough to consider private schools? An on-site Liberated Learners Center, perhaps as an extension of an on-site day care center, could be just the solution.

I can even imagine a youth or family network such as the YMCA, the Scouts, or the Boys and Girls Clubs deciding to use their resources and facilities to offer a school alternative. They are already working with children after school. Perhaps they notice the contrast between how many of their participants trudge through their school day and then how they come alive at their quality programs. They could make their buildings and resources available during the day to improve the lives of children in their communities. They have the experience, the track record, and the capacity to do so.

This vision imagines a rather large philanthropic venture, to offer all teens the possibility of using self-directed learning, instead of being trapped in school until age 18. For certain national businesses and youth networks, the money and coordination might not be so daunting, and we have a relatively simple and efficient model to offer.

One example of this sort of outreach is currently happening with the Boy Scouts in Milton, Massachusetts. A few years ago I spoke with Dan Warren, a homeschooling parent who was also connected to the Scouts. Inspired by our conversation, he has helped to create Home Base, a weekly program for homeschoolers. It meets at the Boy

Scout camp in Milton, and has the support of the facilities and staff of that organization.

Over the past two years, the program has grown to 79 children, and as of 2018, has generated a separate three-day-per-week program as well. Dan is interested in expanding the services just a bit more, so that in addition to serving existing homeschoolers, the program might also work for children and families current-ly attending school, who need some support to consider and embark on homeschooling. The program is going so well that the Boy Scouts are asking Dan to share this approach with at least four other sites around the United States.

This sort of experiment is not unique. Imagine the cultural shift as organizations such as the Scouts use their existing resources to offer year-round, daytime programs with the purpose of offering enough support to provide an option to traditional school. I really believe this sort of expansion is the future, and I look forward to consulting with, cheering on, and celebrating the people and teams involved in this trend.

D. The Dream

I'm trying to be optimistic, and while each of these visions I have laid out are at least plausible, none of them feel particularly imminent. I am glad to share reports of success stories, but I'm not sure we've reached the tip-ping point quite yet. So, where does that leave me, and the North Star concept?

It leaves me thinking. I do have one grand plan that covers all of my bases—my commitment to self-directed learning, my public school roots, my understanding of what teens need to move on to young adulthood, and my con-cerns about efficiency and cost. Are you ready?

Let's turn public schools into North Stars!

I gave a speech outlining this idea at the Thrive 2020 Conference in Guernsey, England, in 2015. The organizer, Marc Winn, challenged me to offer advice on how to make Guernsey the best place on earth to live by 2020. He wanted me to say something more than, "Start a Liberated Learners program in Guernsey." He wanted some creativity.

Okay, I thought to myself. What can I come up with that would be really outrageous, and still be true to myself and my sense of reality? I came up with the following proposal:

My vision is that we keep the schools pretty much as they are. Keep the buildings, keep the teachers, keep the equipment and materials. Let students choose how to use these resources. There would be no judgment, scolding, or pressure on those who used the school program minimally.

Let's keep all the good parts, and just stop with the one thing that is ruining it: treating children as a captive audience.

In summary, I imagine converting the school system into something like a community college system. Teens get six years, ages 13-18, to take the classes they wish. If they complete the distribution requirements of the local school committee, they receive a diploma. If not, they receive a transcript of what they did complete, and they receive some support to obtain a GED.

Students who use the public system only for art, or music, or science, or even sports, are welcome. Some may move on to full-time community college or other activities before they turn age 18.

The building would be an open campus, and students could sit in the library or the cafeteria as students already do at colleges, public libraries, or coffee shops.

Teachers might be able to redesign some of their courses in the ways that college professors can, so instead of ninth grade English, they could offer Poetry or Writing Your Memoir.

There you have it, my best solution. I combine the resources, expertise, and community center functions of the public school with the philosophy of self-directed learning.

Pause for a moment and consider that this proposal would not cost very much money to implement. Schools would feel different, with an open campus, and with every student taking a different course load. Certain rooms might be utilized differently, such as the cafeteria and library. The students' freedom to come and go might feel unnerving to many. But what would it cost? Perhaps nothing.

The staff teaching positions might have to be rearranged or reduced, as some students choose more electives over traditional subjects, and some students attend less than they currently do.

GED preparation might become a standard project for those not planning to do the distribution requirements. Some displaced teachers might become the first set of Advisors needed to supplement the guidance counselors.

In the North Star model, the role of the Advisor is an important part of the process, and having teens reflect regularly on their choices and their progress, while developing a meaningful relationship with an Advisor, is an essential part of our program.

In the speech, I addressed some of the fears and concerns such a change would create. Most of those I've already covered in this book.

Could a public school system adopt such a plan? I suppose a local School Committee that did so would face some pretty tough legal issues with the State Board of Education for not doing their assigned job of compelling students to attend school, and requiring them to follow the mandated state curriculum.

Okay, it's a dream. But not a bad one!

I honored my public school experience, I focused on my self-directed learning career, and I arrived on budget. As a bonus, it's easy to explain and easy to understand. I hereby offer my services to every state's

Board of Education interested in making room for such an experiment.

E. Half A Loaf

I accept that my dream is not realistic, and I have not spent much time discussing it or promoting it outside of the event in Guernsey. I do have a somewhat more realistic plan that addresses students over age 16. Here's how it goes:

During the last week of school in June, the Principal calls the 10th grade class into the auditorium and says:

> *Thank you for making it through tenth grade. Congratulations. You are now 16 years old, the age that compulsory schooling ends in our state. You now have a choice. Those of you who wish to remain with us for two more years are welcomed and encouraged to do so. We have Advanced Placement courses, electives, sports, the prom, and all the things that you know come with being juniors and seniors in high school. We have a high school graduation ceremony and diploma awaiting you. We hope you will stay with us for these opportunities.*

> *If, on the other hand, you feel that you are finished with your use of our services, we support you making an exit at this time. We would like to offer you support to take the GED, enroll at community college, conduct a job search, and get off to a good start in this transition. We will have some guidance counselors-advisors available for you, and I promise there will be no scolding or judgment made about your choice to leave school at this time. Please use our help and keep us posted.*

> *You will remain eligible to play high school sports and participate in our extra-curricular activities. In two years, you may reunite with some of your current high school peers at four-year colleges, with a good number of credits already accrued. Good luck!*

At first, you might think this imaginary speech is preposterous. However, consider that these words are nothing more than an honest public declaration of an already existing truth, one that many people are already acting upon. Many teens throughout the United States are already leaving school early and utilizing community college or engaging in other positive activities without calling themselves "dropouts."

It would be simple to give this speech and to offer the support suggested. It certainly would cost very little to implement. As in my previous vision, any reduction in teaching positions might be offset by shifting some teachers into advisory roles for the students who opt out of school.

I can't actually imagine any local school principal I know uttering this speech and supporting high school students to get a GED, rather than to stay in school through graduation. Any administrator or teacher who actively recommends such behavior for students risks getting fired.

But it is safe for me to say it. And it is safe for all of us to support a teen who wants to get a head start on life by opting out of high school early. I consider this message a highly responsible and inspirational proposal to improve the lives of many teens. Even for those who choose to stay in school, the act of making that choice will dramatically alter how they experience their final two years of high school.

Telling teens the truth—that school is optional—is something we can all start doing right now. Unfortunately, this solution only addresses students over the age of 16 years, and leaves many of the students I've been working with, who are 12-15 years old, trapped in school. Therefore, with some regret, I call it the "half-a-loaf" solution.

F. We are on the right side of history

For those of you who have read this far, I can't leave you with half a solution. It's just not fair, and it's not good enough. So here is my best pep talk for carrying on, each in our own way, with our efforts to make the world a better place:

People involved with the growth of homeschooling over the past twenty to forty years know that many community organizations offer classes and activities for homeschoolers. I'll start by listing some obvious ones, such as libraries, museums, YMCAs, and community colleges. But these familiar places are just the tip of the iceberg. Even in my small town of Montague, Massachusetts, there are dance studios, art spaces, music schools, sports groups, afterschool programs, outdoor education programs, maker spaces, martial arts programs, and homeschooling co-ops. Collectively, these offerings represent a huge range of classes and social opportunities.

There are also religious institutions, ethnic pride groups, and community service organizations that welcome teens. In addition, there is an ever-increasing set of online classes and resources available to people pursuing specific interests. In some communities, the homeschooling offerings are far more than any child could utilize or need. It's sort of like the range of summertime camps and other activities extended year-round.

What if the percentage of the student population utilizing homeschooling continues to grow, from three percent to five percent to eight percent to ten percent? As more families experiment with homeschooling, more and more people will know someone who has tried this approach. The results may be mixed, but overall, we see homeschoolers growing up and attending high school, college, and entering the workforce in generally healthy ways.

What if the camps, afterschool programs, and other youth services providers expand their offerings to this population, and the current impressive range of options doubles or triples or quadruples in the coming years? What if homeschooling co-ops decide to reach out and actively support neighbors who are interested in the model but feel daunted by the responsibilities and practical implementation?

In addition to this expansion, the costs of private schools and college education are pushing many families into the self-directed learning process, without any

reference to the phrase "homeschooling" or any program such as North Star. In fact, our local community
colleges are expanding their outreach to high school-
age students interested in getting an affordable head
start on college.

For many families, the concept of using community college part-time or full-time during the high school
years—with or without the approval of a high school's dual
enrollment program—is common sense. Four years of
private high school and four years of private college might
cost nearly $500,000 in the coming decade. Two years
of community college and two years of public university
might cost ten percent of that figure.

The flexibility of a non-high school lifestyle, combined
with the practicality of these finances, will be making our
approach all the more appealing when contrasted with an
ever-more-stressful, test-based public school experience
that aims for an unaffordable four-year college outcome.
The larger cultural trends are already pushing thoughtful
people in this direction.

Best of all, as I consider the landscape of education reform, all families can choose self-directed learning
without lotteries, waiting lists, or applications for admission. Every family that wants to try this approach can
file a homeschooling plan today and begin the adventure
tomorrow. This truth makes our approach all the more
profound and invigorating.

What if—as in my fondest dreams—the act of not
going to school becomes normalized, accepted and even
downright supported? Not through any deliberate act of
public policy, nor by any dramatic success of North Star
and Liberated Learners…What if it just happens naturally,
with a continuation of these current trends?

What if, in twenty years, a center such as North Star
specifically for self-directed learning, becomes unnecessary?
What if, in the end, by the sheer trajectory of history, North
Star becomes redundant? We already close during the
summer, because opportunities for children in our culture

are so open and abundant then. What if this became the case all year round?

I can imagine this future, perhaps more easily than others. I believe homeschooling is a movement that will continue to grow. The market for teachers and organizations to offer classes during the week for homeschoolers will continue to grow as well.

The homeschooling pioneers of the 1970s and 1980s took risks that have resulted in a movement. Creative entrepreneurs who enjoy working with this community are discovering how to engage with the modern homeschooling movement. The grown homeschoolers are thriving and becoming adults in their communities, and through their role-modeling, active work, and eventual parenting, they will make the movement spread even faster.

I feel that I have a role in this historical trajectory, one that is evolving as the movement grows and changes. My concern remains that this option of self-directed learning be inclusive, and those utilizing it and organizing it expend some effort to make the approach available to their neighbors.

In the long run, I believe this expansion and support for inclusion will happen on its own. This process will play out, and the forces that drive it are far larger than any one person can direct.

But that is a long-term vision. I am curious to see how far it proceeds in my lifetime. For now, I will hope to hear from philanthropists who want to fund centers and public schools that want to work together with us. I will be observing the political movements around School Choice, charters, vouchers, and ESAs to see if any openings arise to benefit self-directed learning. I'll be celebrating the expansion of the independent homeschooling movement and the various programs serving those families.

Mostly, though, I'll be supporting others to use our model and join Liberated Learners, spreading self-directed learning to other communities.

Finally, I'll be working at North Star, meeting with one family at a time, to help them understand their options and offer them the comprehensive support of a program they need to utilize self-directed learning.

I can make today the last day of school for any interested teen in my area. That is the best solution I have for now.

Epilogue

The following essays were contributed by my children, Claudia and Sam. I believe they lend a "view from without" that—while not a part of North Star—provides a uniquely close view that can be more objective, while still being informed. I think their observations round out the views I have put forth in the rest of this book. As of Fall 2018, Claudia is studying at the University of Vermont, and Sam is working with Playworks!, an Americorps program, at an elementary school in Roxbury, Massachusetts.

Claudia

When I was in eighth grade, my dad asked me why school couldn't be like camp.

My immediate response was a look of disbelief, as if he had just appeared from Mars, and then a cynical, "Camp is FUN! (My eyes lit up.) School is, well...school." I went to a summer-long camp for eight consecutive summers, and each one was more exciting than the previous one.

In that moment, my 13-year-old self brushed off this question as a beyond-realistic idea. But the idea that maybe school could be more like camp lingered in the back of my mind, and to this day, it still does.

At camp, I pursued my interests, embraced the challenge-by-choice principle, navigated social scenes, and loved every minute of it. While I certainly had many freedoms at camp, there was still a strong framework and schedule to adhere to.

My dad wanted me to wake up with the same excitement and joy for a school day in January as I did for a day at camp in July. Since he posed the question—why can't school be more like camp?—I wanted to be able to respond positively, to justify going to school in the first place.

Somewhere along the line, as this seemingly preposterous idea lingered in the back of my mind, the language slightly altered, such that I replaced 'school' with 'life.' This seemed like a more tangible and realistic option for me.

For starters, it seemed awfully ridiculous to me that he actually thought his work was like camp; but hey, good for him. But, if my dad could make his daily activities camp-like, why couldn't I? Furthermore, trying to pursue this way of life would be far more joyful for me than anything else I could think of doing at the time.

At camp, we talked a lot about bringing our "camp self" to the "real world." I earnestly thought about this idea and valued these discussions. But my dad's (altered) question posed a different idea. Rather than the individual being the variable, suddenly it's not just about myself, but about the entire world I create for myself. This thinking is more tangible to me.

Being my "camp self" in a school environment with many tasks that held little meaning to me, feeling overcome with obedience training, and spending the day with peers who didn't really enjoy most parts of it, either, was challenging for me.

To create a way of life that extends the camp environment would mean having a lifestyle that includes the same things I do at camp—pursuing interests, embracing challenges and deciding when I'm ready for more, navigating social scenes, and doing these things with joy and enthusiasm.

This vision directly relates to one of North Star's principles: "How people behave under one set of circumstances and assumptions does not predict how they will behave under a very different set of circumstances and assumptions."

For me, during my high school years, this meant:
- choosing to take the honors classes for subjects I was excited about
- playing sports and being one of the captains of the Nordic ski team
- joining clubs
- having a job

- doing an experiential education wilderness semester program with Kroka Expeditions
- interning on a family friend's no-till vegetable farm
- interning with a composting toilet expert
- volunteering at a wilderness program for young home-schoolers
- joining a community climate action group
- taking advantage of some environmentally themed community events nearby at UMASS
- taking all community college classes during my senior year of high school

I am writing this on the tiny island of Kosrae, in Micronesia, where I have spent this year (2017-18) before college interning at Green Banana Paper Company, intimately participating in coral reef conservation projects, and soaking up the island culture.

I can tell you what I did not do or have, including:

- zero AP classes
- no stellar SAT/ACT test scores
- no pre-calculus or trigonometry (I chose statistics instead)
- and no college counselor.

Overall, I still do not find any of these missing items meaningful. Essentially, I chose to say 'no thank you' to making my college applications perfect. Instead, I tried to focus my energy on having a joyful, meaningful, and engaged time throughout high school. When the time came for college applications, I was accepted into the four environmentally themed schools that I applied to, and received merit scholarships from three of them, including an offer of $20,000 per year for four years.

My series of choices were options that many of my peers could do if they want to live this way. I set up internships through word-of-mouth and deciding what I wanted to learn about. Any junior or senior can do dual-enrollment (at least in Massachusetts. I don't know each state's rules). Students who live in the school district can play on the sports teams whether they are attending the public school or homeschooling. The Kroka semester program did have an application and a high tuition, making it the most restrictive activity that I've listed.

My brother, Sam, and I chose to go to school, and we both agreed that we learned far more in one summer at camp than we did in a school year. On the last night of one winter break, our family was out together and Sam lamented, "Aww, I don't want to go to school tomorrow... who needs school anyways?"

I stayed quiet because I was curious how long it would take him to recognize the situation. My dad looked over at him and then it clicked in my brother's head. "Oh, yeah, what? I don't mean that!"

My dad was about to agree with him and offer him the option to stop going to school tomorrow, for the thousandth time. By the time my brother's senior year came around, he was pleading with our dad to just let him graduate high school and go straight to college. He had no interest in a gap year, any more than he had wanted an alternative to high school. It turns out that in 2018, my brother graduated from college in four years, as well.

I enjoyed hearing stories about North Star from my dad, and I appreciated the daily satisfaction and cheerfulness he shared about his work, but I never wanted to be a member of North Star. Still, one of North Star's guiding principles has stuck with me after reading it at The Brunch (Celebration of Self-Directed Learning) year after year, which is, "The best preparation for a meaningful and productive future is a meaningful and productive present."

This is a very inspiring statement for me. It's a simple reassurance that pursuing my interests is just what I need to be doing at the moment. If I am engaged and present in my daily activities and they are meaningful to me, then I am satisfied. I believe learning to seek and create meaningful opportunities is just as important as the activity itself, and definitely something that will always be of value to me.

I write this as a thank-you note to my father:

I heard stories and saw teenagers thriving without school, and I decided I wanted to trust this model— that I could have more joyful and fulfilling days than settling for mediocrity in school. Six years later, I can respond to your question—Why can't school be like camp?—with more than a cynical eye-roll. I've learned that I can say, "I'm not so sure about school yet, but I know that I can create a life with ideas, values, and joy, similar to camp!" And many thanks to you and mom for letting me have as little or as much involvement as I wanted with North Star and self-directed learning.

I have moved on from this aforementioned camp, though there are many philosophies from there that still stick with me today.

I carry on with excitement and joy for what's next: a summer job with Kroka Expeditions, then attending the University of Vermont. I am striving to have a meaningful and productive present, while maintaining balance with a bigger picture. I know that I have the tools and support to continue this pattern of waking up excited to greet the sun. As much as I love to write, I will always struggle to articulate the value of that.

I recognize that my dad's work of coaching teens to leave school is a sensitive subject to many people, and in my personal opinion, often misunderstood. I never chose to be a member at North Star, though I did utilize various aspects of its program throughout high school. I did receive a high school diploma.

I wish for you, reader, that you have the tools to create engagement and joy in a present moment that is meaningful to you, and with minimal stress, especially with the college application process. There's a saying at camp: If you're not having fun, then you're not doing it right!

Sam

Before you read any further, I want to make something crystal clear: My life is nowhere near as radical and adventurous as those of my sister and dad. If you're expecting to read a revolutionary tale of a teenager who said "NO" to the system and paved his own way, I assure you that character is not me. Compared to the life experiences of my sister and Pops, I am burnt toast with butter at best, definitely no jam. Allow me to explain to you my upbringing and experiences:

Many people describe middle and high school as the worst years of their lives, recalling stories of getting stuffed in lockers, beat up on the playground, and playing the victim role of many school-wide jokes. Luckily, I only got put in a locker once (more of a test to see if I could fit), and I was the butt of only a few jokes with my friends. My time in high school was actually enjoyable and I have many fond memories of the time spent there.

For me, the toughest part about high school was waking up at the ridiculous hour of 6:30 a.m.—wondering why any sane human being would do this—and dragging myself into the shower, knowing that if I didn't hurry up, I'd miss the bus. Thankfully, the bus driver was a kind man, and I only missed it a few times.

Growing up, I stayed at the same private elementary school until I graduated sixth grade, and then transitioned to the public school system for middle and high school. I had met many friends playing little league baseball, and wanted to go to school with them rather than attend a private school.

After transitioning to the public school system of Montague, I happily spent my time in middle school goofing around, playing sports, and forming friendships which I hold to this day. Upon completion of middle school, I had full intentions of continuing on to high school at Turners Falls, where I spent four more satisfactory years until I graduated in 2014.

Looking back, I can appreciate that these years were kind to me, and that not everyone is as fortunate as I was to be in a place where they are content and happy.

I've heard the North Star spiel so many times that I could probably recite it in my sleep at this point. "If you don't like school, stop going."

As a teenager, I stopped listening to my Dad after this phrase was said, because as absurd and preposterous as this might sound, I actually enjoyed school, or at least didn't mind it.

Some of the best memories of my life come from high school, such as playing on my high school football team, the Turners Falls Indians. The chemistry which grew between that group of guys was largely because we spent so much time together; at practice, in school, and out of school. It's completely possible that I could have home-schooled and still participated on the team. However, I never felt the desire to homeschool because I was happy and content with my situation at school.

The final message I want to suggest is that if you are unhappy with something, change it!

I work at a summer camp called Lanakila, where we practice a model of counseling called success counseling. In the psychology world, this is quite similar to a model of thought titled Choice Theory.

Success counseling structure is built upon several foundational questions, the first three of which are most applicable to this example. If you are unhappy in school, life, or any situation, I urge you to ask yourself these questions:

- What do you want?
- What are you doing to get it?
- Is it working?
- What is one step you can take to make the situation better than it is, right now?

When my Dad made the statement, "If you don't like school, stop going," I stopped listening because I already had what I wanted. I enjoyed being with my friends at school and felt no desire to change this situation. My experience was pleasant rather than unpleasant, and I generally felt positive about school. I wanted to be happy, and that desire was being met.

For those people stuck in school feeling unhappy, perhaps there are different avenues you can explore to become a happier, more wholesome individual.

If staying in school isn't working, there are plenty of other opportunities, and you have the power to choose your path. Perhaps that one step forward toward making the situation better is less drastic than leaving school, and could include joining a new sports team, participating in after-school activities, or taking different classes.

Or perhaps the situation has reached a point where it's time for a new path to be blazed. Shoot, now I sound like my dad.

Anyway, the point is that if you feel unhappy about your situation in school, life, or with a relationship, you have the power to change that feeling by taking intentional steps to make the situation better.

Throughout the course of my education, I felt no desire to homeschool, as I was pleased with the situations I was in. While I never got to live on a tropical island in Micronesia or go Nordic skiing for weeks in sub-zero weather in Canada (to this day, I question my sister's sanity for doing that), I have lifelong friends from high school and many fond memories which I will take to the grave.

I am lucky for that, and I wouldn't change a thing.

Author's Note

Claudia and Sam have shared their own experiences of being offered a range of educational options, and having the determination to make the most of their choices. This responsibility and maturity is what I wish for all teens.

I did not need or push for my children to choose North Star, and I do not urge all teens who visit North Star for that first conversation to leave school. I want all teens to know they have some choices about how they spend their time and energy regarding schooling, and that North Star offers one option they may not have considered before.

As my children move on to college and the adult work world, I hope they carry with them the sense of independence and self-control they portray in their writing, and that I have attributed to many North Star alumni in this book.

What more could a parent want?

Appendix 1

Sample Alumna Transcript: Raphaela Levy-Moore

Cumulative GPA for all college classes: 4.0
College credits: 50

Test Scores

SAT I: 1510
780 Math
730 Verbal

SAT II:
790 Writing
720 Literature
700 Math IC

LIST OF CLASSES, GRADES 10-12

10th Grade

Frequently Banned Books
This course included explorations into the cultural contexts in which these books were written, as well as the history of the censorship laws surrounding them.
- *One Flew Over The Cuckoo's Nest,* Ken Kesey
- *East of Eden,* John Steinbeck
- *Of Mice and Men,* John Steinbeck
- *Fahrenheit451,* Ray Bradbury

- *The Adventures of Huckleberry Finn*, Mark Twain
- *The Bluest Eye*, Toni Morrison
- *Johnny Got His Gun*, Dalton Trumbo
- *Slaughterhouse Five*, Kurt Vonnegut
- *Stranger in a Strange Land*, Robert Heinlein
- *The Picture of Dorian Gray*, Oscar Wilde

Political Books, Cultural Criticism and Philosophy
- *The Cointelpro Papers*, Ward Churchill & Jim Vander Wall
- *No Pity*, Joseph Shapiro
- *Jihad vs. McWorld*, Benajmin R. Barber
- *The Zapatista Reader*, Tom Hayden
- *Iraq Under Siege: The Deadly Impact of Sanctions and War*, Anthony Arnove, Editor
- *War Is A Force That Gives Us Meaning*, Chris Hedges
- *The Best Democracy Money Can Buy*, Greg Palast
- *Sweatshop Warriors*, Miriam Ching Yoon Louie
- *Anarchism and Other Essays*, Emma Goldman
- *Why I Am Not A Christian*, Bertrand Russell

Beat Literature
- *The Portable Beat Reader*, Ann Charters, Editor
- *On The Road*, Jack Kerouac
- *The Dharma Bums*, Jack Kerouac
- *Visions of Gerard*, Jack Kerouac
- *Junky*, William Burroughs
- *Naked Lunch*, William Burroughs
- *Nova Express*, William Burroughs
- *Howl and Other Poems*, Allen Ginsberg
- *Death and Fame*, Allen Ginsberg
- *Pieces of a Song*, Diane Di Prima
- *Starting From San Francisco*, Lawrence Ferlinghetti

Utopian/Dystopian Literature
- *The Kin of Ata Are Waiting For You*, Dorothy Bryant
- *Utopia*, Thomas More
- *Island*, Aldous Huxley
- *Looking Backwards*, Edward Bellamy

- *Herland,* Charlotte Perkins Gilman
- *1984,* George Orwell
- *Animal Farm,* George Orwell
- *Brave New World,* Aldous Huxley
- *Brave New World Revisited,* Aldous Huxley
- *The Handmaid's Tale,* Margaret Atwood
- *A Clockwork Orange,* Anthony Burgess
- *Anthem,* Ayn Rand

J.D. Salinger
- *Franny and Zooey*
- *Raise High the Roofbeam Carpenters and Seymour; An Introduction*
- *The Catcher in the Rye*
- *9 Stories*

Adventure Literature
- *Don Quixote,* Miguel de Cervantes
- *Gulliver's Travels,* Jonathan Swift

Creative Writing
This included a short story writing, memoirs, essays, descriptive narratives, etc. We had group critiques and in-class sharing, as well. A great deal of my creative writing was done on my own initiative and with the help of my mother, as well.

Media Studies
Media and Culture, Richard Campbell

Sustainable Communities
- *Gaviotas: A Village to Reinvent the World,* Alan Weisman
- *Sustainable Community Development: Studies in Economic, Environmental, and Cultural Revitalization,* Marie D. Hoff
- *The Ecology of Place: Planning for Environment, Economy, and Community,* Timothy Beatley & Kristy Manning

American History Through the Eyes of the Underrepresented
- *A People's History of the United States,* Howard Zinn
- *The Rise and Fall of the American Teenager,* Thomas Hine
- *The Letters of Sacco and Vanzetti*

Geometry

Biology
I used the fourth edition of *Biology: Life on Earth* by Audesirk in this study. I also read Edward O. Wilson's newest edition of *The Diversity of Life.*

Education Theory
- *The Teenage Liberation Handbook,* Grace Llewellyn
- *Teach Your Own,* John Holt

Figure Drawing

11th Grade

Women's Lives, Women's Stories (H)
Women's literature course taught at Hampshire College

Ancient Greek and Indian Drama (H)
Study of ancient Greek and Sanskrit drama at Hampshire College. This course, in many ways, was what made me fall in love with the classics and inspired me to study Latin.

Prison Literature
I was inspired to study both the writings of prisoners and the social and spiritual commentaries about their plights, because the prison industry has been growing at a shocking rate and I felt that I couldn't ignore the voices of so many prisoners.
- *We're All Doing Time,* Bo Lozoff
- *The Executioner's Song,* Norman Mailer
- *Live From Death Row,* Mumia Abu-Jamal

- *Prison Writings: My Life Is My Sun Dance,* Leonard Peltier
- *No More Prisons,* William Upsky Wimsatt

Shakespeare

This class included an exploration into Shakespear's trag-
edies, comedies, histories and sonnets. It also involved
memorization of monologues and scenes for recitation during North Star events.

- *Romeo and Juliet*
- *Hamlet*
- *Othello*
- *Macbeth*
- *The Merchant of Venice*
- *The Tempest*
- *The Taming of the Shrew*
- *A Midsummer Night's Dream*
- *Julius Caesar*
- *Antony and Cleopatra*
- *The Sonnets of William Shakespeare*

Russian Literature

- *Notes from the Underground,* Fyodor Dostoevsky
- *The Idiot,* Fyodor Dostoevsky
- *Demons,* Fyodor Dostoevsky
- *Crime and Punishment,* Fyodor Dostoevsky
- *The Brothers Karamazov,* Fyodor Dostoevsky
- *War and Peace,* Leo Tolstoy
- *The Kreutzer Sonata and Other Stories,* Leo Tolstoy
- *Anna Karenina,* Leo Tolstoy
- *Dead Souls,* Nikolai Gogol
- *The Overcoat and Other Stories,* Nikolai Gogol

Sexuality and Sexual Deviance

- *Fear of Flying,* Erica Jong
- *Juliette,* Marquis de Sade
- *City of Night,* John Rechy
- *Lolita,* Vladimir Nabokov
- *Rubyfruit Jungle,* Rita Mae Brown

French Romanticism
- *Les Miserables*, Victor Hugo
- *The Count of Monte Cristo*, Alexandre Dumas

Women Writers
- *The Bell Jar*, Sylvia Plath
- *A Tree Grows in Brooklyn*, Betty Smith
- *Surfacing*, Margaret Atwood
- *Wuthering Heights*, Emily Bronte
- *To Kill a Mockingbird*, Harper Lee
- *The Color Purple*, Alice Walker

Social Issues
- *War Talk*, Arundhati Roy
- *The Iraq War Reader: History, Documents, Opinions*, Micah L. Sifry and Christopher Cerf
- *Perpetual War for Perpetual Peace*, Gore Vidal

Intensive Elementary Latin 126 (UMASS)
This was a 6-credit intensive Latin course that covered two semesters' worth of Latin in 6 weeks.

Intensive Intermediate Latin 246 (UMASS)
This was a second 6-credit intensive Latin course that covered two semesters' worth of Latin in 6 weeks. I enjoyed both of these courses tremendously, and would have loved to continue studying advanced Latin at UMASS, but scheduling difficulties prohibited me from doing so. I have continued the study on my own, however, and plan to officially resume it once I am matriculated into college as a degree-seeking candidate.

12th Grade

Human Ecology 101 (GCC)
Cultural Anthropology 104 (GCC)
English 101 (GCC)
College Algebra 107 (GCC)

Greek History, Philosophy, Drama and Myth
After taking a course in Greek and Indian Drama at
Hampshire College, I fell in love with Greek theater and
Greek mythology. The books listed below were read on my
own after the course had ended. I particularly fell in love
with the works of Euripides, and this is heavily reflected in
my choice of dramas. This passion eventually led me to
lead a class of Greek Drama at North Star, and I think that
it also set the stage for my interest in Roman history and
the Latin language.
- *The Histories*, Herodotus
- *The Life of Alexander the Great*, Plutarch
- *Women in Greek Myth*, Mary Lefkowitz
- *The Republic*, Plato
- *Prometheus Bound*, Aeschylus
- *Elektra*, Sophocles
- *Philoctetes*, Sophocles
- *Medea*, Euripides
- *Iphigenia at Aulis*, Euripides
- *Iphigenia at Tauris*, Euripides
- *Elektra*, Euripides
- *Hippolytus*, Euripides
- *Trojan Women*, Euripides
- *Alcestis*, Euripides
- *Lysistrata*, Aristophanes
- *Frogs*, Aristophanes
- *The Greek Way to Western Civilization*, Edith Hamilton

Roman History, Literature, and the Latin Language
In the summer of 2004, I studied Latin intensively at the
University of Massachusetts. Scheduling difficulties pre-
vented me from pursuing the study at UMASS, but I loved
Latin too much to give it up. I am currently teaching a
class in Latin at North Star, and would love to major in the
classics.
- *The Assassination of Julius Caesar: A People's History
  of Ancient Rome*, Michael Parenti
- *Fall of the Roman Republic*, Plutarch

- *De Bello Gallico,* Caesar (read primarily in Latin)
- *Odes,* Horace (readings in both English and Latin)
- *Latin in Oxford, Inscriptiones Aliquot Oxonienses,* Reginald H. Allen
- *The Art of Love,* Ovid (read in both Latin and English)
- *The Aeneid,* Virgil
- *The Four Orations Against Cataline,* Cicero (read in both Latin and English)
- *The Seven Remaining Orations,* Cicero (read in both Latin and English)

Environmental Problems and Solutions
- *Eco-Economy,* Lester R. Brown
- *The Sea Around Us,* Rachel Carson
- *Silent Spring,* Rachel Carson
- *Every Drop For Sale,* Jeffrey Rothfeder
- *The Legacy of Luna,* Julia Butterfly Hill
- *One Makes the Difference,* Julia Butterfly Hill
- *Sustainable Agriculture and Resistance,* Fernando Funes and Luis Garcia

Basic Studio/Drawing (UMASS)
This was an intensive 22.5-hour weekly art course during January 2005, taught at UMASS. We used a variety of media to replicate the human figure, and still life and landscapes.

Sociology 101 (GCC)
Pre-Calculus 108 (GCC)
Environmental Ethics (GCC)

Ancient Wilderness Living Skills (GCC)
This was a three-day, two-night camping trip through GCC, where we learned how to build debris shelters to sleep in without a sleeping bag; create fire by rubbing sticks together; make rope by twisting milkweed; carve spoons; and many other ancient wilderness living skills.

Sustainable Agriculture/Organic Gardening

This was another one-credit workshop class offered through Greenfield Community College, where we visited local farms and gardens, and helped out with them. We also read about agriculture and particularly the sustainable agricultural transformation in Cuba. Growing my own food has always been something very important for me.

Ecological Living and Sustainable Development

I have always loved art, and for the past few years, that has manifested itself through my love of architecture. At first, it seemed difficult to reconcile a love for designing buildings—which as a whole, creates so much waste and wreaks havoc on the environment—with my equally passionate feelings for the earth and the necessity to live sustainably.

When I was young, even before I understood about ecologically friendly design and development, I understood the need to find alternatives. My passion for sustainable architecture opened up a lot of new interests, such as vernacular architecture, building with earth, permaculture, and organic gardening and farming. It also led me to participate in numerous natural building and permaculture classes and workshops. Reading included:

- *Built By Hand,* Bill Steen
- *Cradle to Cradle: Remaking the Way We Make Things,* Michael Braungart and William McDonough
- *Shelter,* Lloyd Kahn
- *Home Work: Handbuilt Shelter,* Lloyd Kahn
- *Tree Houses by Architects,* James Grayson Trulove
- *Green By Design: Creating a Home for Sustainable Living,* Angela M. Dean
- *Sustainable Homes,* James Grayson Trulove
- *The Solar Home,* Mark Freeman
- *The Hand-Sculpted House,* Ianto Evans & Michael G. Smith
- *Dwelling,* Paul Oliver
- *Present Value: Constructing a Sustainable Future,* Gigi Coe

- *Saunders Shrewsbury House,* W.A. Shurcliff
- *The First Passive Solar Home Awards,* Franklin Research Center
- *Maine Solar Architecture: A Building Inventory,* The Maine Office of Energy Resources
- *Solar Dwelling Design Concepts*, The AIA Research Corp.
- *The Art of Natural Building: Design, Structure, Resources,* Joseph F. Kennedy and Michael Smith
- *The New Ecological Home: A Complete Guide to Green Building Options*, Dan Chiras
- *The New Natural House Book,* Pearson
- *The Natural House,* Chiras
- *The Good House Book,* Clark Snell

Feminist Writings and Viewpoints
- *Subject to Debate: Sense and Dissents on Women, Politics, and Culture,* Katha Pollitt
- *The Beauty Myth,* Naomi Wolf
- *The W Effect: Bush's War on Women*, Laura Flanders
- *Body Outlaws*, Ophira Edut
- *Intercourse,* Andrea Dworkin
- *Against Our Will: Men, Women, and Rape*, Susan Brownmiller
- *The War on Choice*, Gloria Feldt
- *Female Chauvinist Pigs: Women and the Rise of Raunch Culture*, Arile Levy
- *Transforming a Rape Culture,* Emile Buchwald, Pamela R. Fletcher, and Martha Roth

Calculus and Analytical Geometry
Saxon

Physics
Saxon
- *The Birth of a New Physics,* I. Bernard Cohen

Mathematical History, Special Numbers, and Number Theory
- *Fermat's Enigma,* Simon Singh and John Lynch

- *The Golden Ratio,* Mario Livio
- *The Principles of Mathematics,* Bertrand Russell
- *Q.E.D.: Beauty in Mathematical Proof,* Burkard Polster
- *Selections from Euclid's Thirteen Books of the Elements,* Euclid

South African Literature
- *Waiting for the Barbarians,* J.M. Coetzee
- *Life and Times of Michael K.,* J.M. Coetzee
- *Disgrace,* J.M. Coetzee
- *Age of Iron,* J.M. Coetzee
- *July's People,* Nadine Gordimer

Recently read:
- *Moravagine,* Blaise Cendrars
- *One Hundred Years of Solitude,* Gabriel Garcia Marquez
- *Catch-22,* Joseph Heller
- *The Poisonwood Bible,* Barbara Kingsolver
- *Victoria,* Knut Hamsen

Brazil Trip, Summer 2005, 35 Days
Permaculture (University of Massachusetts)
This was a UMASS course affiliated with the Living Routes program that was taught for three weeks in Brazil. The studying and work involved was intensive, centered around permaculture land design, ecological building, animal care, and planting. The text for this course was Bill Mollison's *Introduction to Permaculture,* and we were very blessed to actually have him there with us, teaching us about permaculture himself. I have also begun to read a lot of permaculture-related literature on my own, such as *Gaia's Garden: A Guide to Home-Scale Permaculture,* by Tom Hemenway. This was a 130-hour course that ended with my certification as a permaculture apprentice. I also spent time volunteering at an ecovillage in Brazil, as well.

Biocontsruindo
Bioconstruindo was a week-long extension of the Permaculture course in Brazil. It was a mainly hands-on

course, devoted to the building of structures using sustainable, natural materials and techniques. During this course, we worked with cob, adobe, superadobe earth bags, bamboo, soil cement, straw bale, stone, and other forms of natural construction.

Portugese Language
I took Portugese lessons while in Brazil, immersed myself in Portugese-speaking environments, and also studied it on my own, using the *Teach Yourself Portugese* book and CD, and *501 Portugese Verbs.*

Iceland Trip, Summer 2005, 20 days
Worked on a nature reserve near Reykjavik from September 1-20. Used the *Teach Yourself Icelandic* book and CD in order to learn the language. Also read *The Icelandic Sagas* and studied Icelandic culture and literary traditions.

Thailand Trip, Autumn 2005, 28 days
I spent four weeks in a town called Ayutthaya, where I helped care for disadvantaged children and taught the English language to Thai people. In my free time, I also tutored a young Thai boy in English.

New Zealand Trip, Autumn 2005, 28 days
I participated in a Habitat for Humanity Global Village Trip for two weeks, then spent another two weeks exploring the South Island on my own. While volunteering with Habitat, I aided in the construction of two homes for low-income Maori families.

Chile Trip, Winter 2005, 28 days
I spent four weeks in Chile, where I studied Spanish intensively for a total of 67 hours at Bridge-Linguatec. In the afternoons, I volunteered at an orphanage and cared for abandoned Chilean infants, for a total of 60 hours.

ACTIVITIES LIST

Volunteer at North Star – Teaching Latin, Greek Drama, leading Feminist Discussion. I taught three classes at North Star; two were official weekly classes, and the third was an informal, twice-weekly feminist discussion. I also tutored people in various subjects. In my Greek Drama class, we read and discussed the works of Aeschylus, Sophocles and Euripides. In my Latin class, I taught the basic fundamentals of grammar and a bit of Roman history. We also translated poems and orations together. My Feminist Theory class was centered around late-20th century feminist issues, and various subcategories within the feminist movement.

North Star Board of Directors, 2003-2004. I was honored to be asked to join the Board of Directors at North Star. Due to scheduling difficulties, I had to leave, but have remained active with North Star events.

North Star Children's Group, teaching art classes and supervising homeschooled children. I taught a weekly art class to homeschooled children. In this class, we did sculpture, painting, origami, knitting, and various other arts and crafts projects.

Appendix 2

Alumni Achievements

Reprinted from: "What Happens to Self-Directed Learners?" by Kenneth Danford, published in Tipping Points, *the online magazine of the Alliance for Self-Directed Education (Feb. 16, 2017).*

Following are lists of specific community colleges, four-year colleges, certificate or training programs, and work experiences of North Star alumni. These lists include outcomes from alumni in both Report One and Report Two, mentioned in Chapter 11.

HIGHER EDUCATION

Community Colleges and Certificate or Training Programs

Those places with two or more alumni have the number in parentheses; those with more than five are at the top.

> Greenfield Community College, Massachusetts (94)
> Holyoke Community College, Massachusetts (60)
>
> American Musical and Dramatic Academy, New York
> Berkeley City College, California
> Berklee online, Massachusetts
> Berkshire Community College, Massachusetts (2)
> Boston Dance Company, Massachusetts
> Branford Hall, Connecticut
> Bunker Hill Community College, Massachusetts

Cabinetry Training, Massachusetts
Cabrillo College, California
California College of the Arts, California
Central Pennsylvania Youth Ballet, Pennsylvania
City College of San Francisco, California
Community College of Connecticut
Community College of Vermont
Concordia College Montreal, Canada
Cosmetology Certificate, Massachusetts
Connecticut Center for Massage Therapy
Culinary Institute of America, New York
EMT Training
Flatiron School, New York
GCC Outdoor Leadership Program, Massachusetts
Hallmark School of Photography, Massachusetts
Harvard Community Extension, Massachusetts (2)
Johnson College, Tennessee
Kapiolani Community College, Hawaii
Landing School of Boatbuilding, Massachusetts
Landmark College, Vermont
Le Cordon Bleu, France
Maine College of Art
Maine School of Masonry
Marinello Cosmetology, Massachusetts
Massage Training (2)
Middlesex Community College, Massachusetts
Midwifery Training
Millersville Community College, Tennessee
New England School of Photography, Massachusetts
North Shore Community College Massachusetts
Northwestern Connecticut Community College
New York Institute of Photography
Royal Winnipeg Ballet Academy, Alberta, Canada
Sage Mountain Herbal, Vermont
Santa Barbara City College, California
Simon's Rock College, Massachusetts
Springfield Technical Community College, Mass. (2)
TEFL in Nicaragua

Train Engineer Certificate, Massachusetts
Tunxis Community College, Connecticut

Americorps (2)
Peace Corps
Air Force
Army
Coast Guard
Marines

Four-Year College

University of Massachusetts Amherst (49)
Hampshire College, Massachusetts (9)
Mount Holyoke College, Massachusetts (7)

Amherst College, Massachusetts (2)
Antioch, Ohio
Art Institute of Boston, Massachusetts
Bard College, New York
Bates College, Maine
Becker College, Massachusetts
Beloit College, Wisconsin (2)
Bennington College, Vermont (2)
Brandeis University, Massachusetts
Brown University, Rhode Island (2)
Bryn Mawr College, Pennsylvania
California State University Los Angeles
Central CT State University
Clark University, Massachusetts (2)
Colorado State University (2)
Columbia University, New York
Earlham College, Indiana (2)
East Tennessee State University
Emerson College, Massachusetts (2)
Evergreen State University, Washington
Fashion Institute of Technology, New York
Framingham State, Massachusetts
Goddard College, Vermont

Green Mountain College, Vermont (2)
Guilford College, North Carolina
Haverford College, Pennsylvania
Ithaca College, New York
Lehigh University, Pennsylvania
Lesley College, Massachusetts (2)
Lyme Academy of Fine Arts, Connecticut
Macalester College, Minnesota
Maine College of Art
Manhattan School of Music, New York
Marlboro College, Vermont
Massachusetts College of Art and Design
Massachusetts College of Liberal Arts (2)
Massachusetts Institute of Technology
Mitchell College, Connecticut
Montserrat School of Fine Arts, Massachusetts
New York University
Newbury College, Massachusetts
Northeastern University, Massachusetts (2)
Pitzer College, California
Reed College, Oregon
Rhode Island School of Design (2)
Sarah Lawrence University, New York
Shimer College, Illinois
Smith College, Massachusetts (2)
Southern New Hampshire University
Springfield College, Massachusetts (3)
St. John's College, New Mexico
Sterling College, Vermont
Texas A&M University
The New School, New York
Unity College, Maine
University of Alaska
University of Auckland, New Zealand
University of Colorado
University of Massachusetts Boston
University of Massachusetts Dartmouth
University of Massachusetts Lowell

University of Southern Maine
University of Vermont
Warren Wilson College, North Carolina (3)
Wellesley College, Massachusetts
Westfield State University, Massachusetts
Whitman College, Washington
Williams College, Massachusetts (2)
Worcester Polytechnic Institute, Massachusetts

Graduate School Programs

Berklee College of Music, Massachusetts
Brandeis University, Massachusetts
Brown University, Rhode Island
Endicott College, Massachusetts
Fordham University School of Law, New York
Fordham University MFA, New York
Fulbright Scholar in Jordan
Hartt Music, Connecticut
Indiana University, Indiana
Lesley University, Massachusetts (3)
Lincoln College of New England
London Academy of Music and Dramatic Art
London School of Economics
Middlebury College, Vermont
Rice University, Texas (2)
School of International Training, Vermont
Simmons College, Massachusetts
Smith College of Social Work, Massachusetts
UCLA Thelonius Monk Institute, California
UMass Medical School
Universidad Rafael Landivar, Guatemala
University of California Berkeley
University of Chicago, Illinois
University of Colorado, Colorado Springs
University of Connecticut (2)
University of Kentucky
University of Massachusetts (5)
University of Washington

Victoria University, Wellington, New Zealand
Watson Fellowship, Bryn Mawr, Pennsylvania
Westfield State University, Massachusetts
Yale Law School, Connecticut

CAREERS

Entrepreneurial
Alternative Energy Business
Antiques Dealer
Artist (5)
Auto Repair
Carpenter (3)
Cartoonist
Cell Phone Sales
Childcare
Comedian
Computer Animation
Copy Editing
Craftsperson
Custom Gowns
Dog Day Care
Filmmaking
Generator Systems
Green Cleaning Business
Horse Shows
Illustrator
International Business
Jewelry Making
Labor Activist
Landscaping (2)
Massage Therapist
Music DJ
Music Recording Studio
Musician (7)
Painter
Photography (6)
Pilates Instructor

Pottery
Puppeteer
Restaurants
Shared Business Space
Software Engineer
Summer Camps
Theatre Company
Yoga Instructor

Unusual Work
Acting
Art
Buddhist Monk in Japan
Circus
Glassblowing
Fashion Design
Hair Design
Homesteading
Horse Breeding, Training
Make-Up Artist
Mindfulness
Mixed Martial Arts
Music Composer
Rock Climbing
Tennis
Travel
Yacht Repair

Professional Positions
Acrisure Insurance
Adafruit, Apple
Art Education
Art Teacher
Astrocamp
Ballet
Big Y, Department Manager, River Valley Market
Biostatistician Seattle Children's Hospital
Boat Builder

Business Consultant
Business Manager
Chef
Chemist, PPG Industries
Community Cable TV Manager
Computer Networker
Computer Programmer (2)
Costumer, Metropolitan Opera
Counseling at UMass
Counselor, Gandara Center
Daycare Teacher
Doctor, Brigham, RI
EMT
EMT, American Medical Response
Engineer, Wind Turbines, Pika
English Professor
Farmer
Freight Train Conductor
Greenfield Recycling
Hairdresser
Halliburton, Bloomberg
Health Care Information Technology
History Work
Hospitality Work (2)
Human Resources
HVAC
ISO Engineering
Journalist, Al-Jazeera English
Journalist, Majority Report
Journalist, Southern Magazine
JP Morgan Chase
Justice Resource Institute
Labor and Community Activist
Labor Organizing Unite Here
Law Clerk, Federal 9th Circuit Court of Appeals
Librarian, Arlington Public Library
Librarian, GCC
Librarian, Hampshire College

Manager of Cape Cod Inn, Restaurant, Catering
Manager, Green Love Eco Clean
Manager, Roadhouse Restaurant
Masonry
Mortician, CAN
Music and Arts Teaching
Nurse
Nutritionist
PCA, Dementia
Pilates, Physical Therapy
Professor, University of Michigan
Psychologist
Puppeteer
Reading Specialist, Watertown
Sawicki Real Estate
Snow Farm Crafts Education Director
Snow Farm, Starworks
Social Worker
Software Developer
Software Engineer (3)
Software Programming
Staff, North Star
Superintendent of Public Schools, Greenfield MA
Symantec-Dell
Teacher, Spain
Teacher, Students with Disabilities
Teaching Art, YMCA and Camp
Translator, Chinese magazine
U.S. Fish and Wildlife
USDA
Valley Free Radio, Daily Hampshire Gazette
Verite
Verizon Sales
Videographer for Rap Artist Mike Stud
Warner Brothers
Wayfinder Experience
Web Developer, Yiddish Book Center
Youth Work

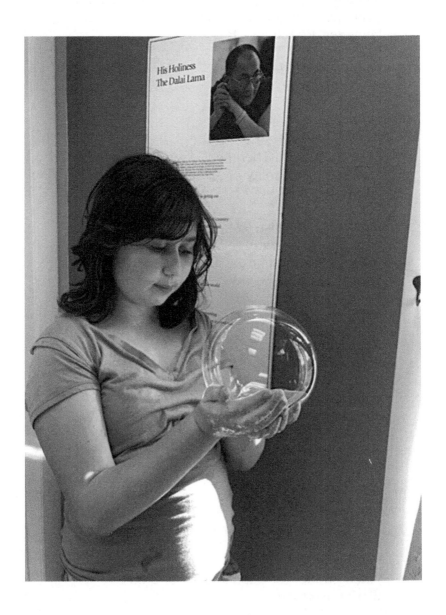

Appendix 3

End Notes

Chapter 4

SGORR: http://www.shaker.org/sgorr.aspx

Coalition of Essential Schools:
http://essentialschools.org/common-principles/

Rethinking Schools: https://rethinkingschools.org

Sudbury Valley Schools: http://sudval.org

Chapter 5

Supreme Court Cases:
http://a2zhomeschooling.com/laws/homeschool_laws_
legalities/homeschooling_court_cases/

Chapter 6

Author's Blog Piece about Camp: https://www.huffington-
post.com/entry/we-love-camp-can-we-love-_b_1627863.html

North Star Calendar:
http://www.northstarteens.org/calendar-and-classes/

Steve Theberge: http://www.stevetheberge.com

Chapter 8

LightHouse Holyoke: http://lighthouseholyoke.org

Jen Eckard:
https://www.youtube.com/watch?v=QSdTdDl512k&list=PL
1ZnHEFAqxxnlbQfgVDSzBXhZU4d4i08H&index=4

Ben Rosser: http://www.benrosser.com

Chapter 9

What are Restorative Practices:
https://www.iirp.edu/what-we-do/defining-restorative/

International Institute for Restorative Practices:
https://www.iirp.edu

Institute for Musical Arts: http://www.ima.org

People to Watch: The Next Generation:
https://www.facebook.com/peopletowatchwesternmass/?fref=nf

Chapter 10

North Star Alumni Outcomes:
https://www.self-directed.org/tp/north-star-alumni/

Alliance for Self-Directed Education:
https://www.self-directed.org

Author's Speech at Thrive 2020, Guernsey, England:
https://www.youtube.com/watch?v=pMb9KJxNi1k

Laura Ross:
https://www.youtube.com/watch?v=jlsXsRSGL-k&t=11s

Eighth Grade Out! Blog Post:
https://www.huffingtonpost.com/kenneth-danford/eighth-grade-out_b_1501461.html

Chapter 11

Princeton Learning Cooperative:
http://princetonlearningcooperative.org

Derek Sivers:
https://www.youtube.com/watch?v=RXMnDG3QzxE

Joel Hammon Tedx Talk:
https://www.youtube.com/watch?v=WuRCUF_XAj0&

Alternative Education Resource Organization:
http://www.educationrevolution.org

Liberated Learners: http://www.educationrevolution.org

Author's Blog Post about 2018 trip to Manila, The
Philippines and Abot Tala:
http://liberatedlearners.net/going-global-liberated-learners-philippines/

Chapter 12

Unschool, San Juan Unified School District, California:
https://www.sanjuan.edu/unschool

Powderhouse Studios, Massachusetts:
https://powderhouse.org

Vouchers:
https://www.edweek.org/ew/issues/vouchers/index.html

United States Supreme Court on Vouchers:
https://www.edweek.org/ew/articles/2002/06/27/
42voucher_web.h21.html

Washington Post article on vouchers:
https://www.washingtonpost.com/local/education/how-indianas-school-voucher-program-soared-and-what-it-says-about-education-in-the-trump-era/2016/12/26/13d1d3ec-bc97-11e6-91ee-1adddfe36cbe_story.html

New Hampshire Education Savings Accounts: http://www.
vnews.com/ESA-Families-14998301

Class Dismissed: http://classdismissedmovie.com

Home School Legal Defense Association on vouchers:
https://www.hslda.org/docs/news/2017/201703010.asp

Workspace Education: http://workspaceeducation.org

Home Base, Boy Scouts of America:
https://www.newenglandbasecamp.org/home-base/

Michigan Homeschool Partnerships Example, Gull Lake
Partnership: http://www.gulllakeschools.net

Acknowledgments

It's one thing to have a story to tell, a second thing to write it all down in a serious way, and entirely a third thing to spin that writing into a book. For more than two decades, I have felt daunted by these steps. I liked telling stories, but writing a book felt like far too much of a process for me to imagine completing.

I appreciate those who have encouraged me to write this book, primarily Joel Hammon, Gary Bernhard, and Joshua Hornick. Joel showed me the way by completing his own book, *The Teacher Liberation Handbook*, essentially challenging me to get on with my own process.

Gary was the first careful reader of each chapter, and his support was a central contribution as those chapters piled up into a coherent set. Joshua knew from the beginning that I had a book-length story to tell, and his persistent yet patient inquiries about the idea of a book have been a core part of my considerations to take on this project.

This book took on life in response to the unbridled enthusiasm of Ted Wachtel, who read the early drafts and replied with, "Right on! Fantastic! Bring on the next chapter!"

Ted introduced me to Mary Shafer, who has led me through the process of taking a manuscript and turning it into a genuine book. Mary's professional and confident guidance has turned what felt like an unknowable and overwhelming process into a step-by-step, guided adventure that I'm told is only just beginning when this book becomes tangible.

I am also grateful for Loran Saito's artistic vision and commitment to making this book cover joyful and inspiring. Seeing the book cover for the first time was a lifetime memory for me.

Along the way, I've shared the draft with many people who have offered detailed and insightful feedback, including: Jon Lackman, Susannah Sheffer, Janney Simpson, Peter Bergson, Amy Rose, Kate Friedman, and Alicia Chin-Gibbons. I appreciate Alison Snieckus for her thorough and careful last-minute edits that polished the final draft.

I remain grateful that each of these people were willing to spend a few hours critically reading my chapters, and I am certain this finished product is better for all of this input.

I also want to acknowledge all of the teens and parents whose stories appear in this book. I have used real names, and all of these people have read the passages about their experiences and allowed me to include them in this work. Their permission to use their names makes a huge difference to me in the power of this book.

This book is largely about providing non-judgmental support to teens, to help them identify and follow their dreams. In my personal life, I thank Zachary Green and Marcia Jaffee, who first taught me these skills and inspired me towards a career in teaching and counseling.

I have been the recipient of love and unconditional support from many people, most importantly my wife, Tamara Kaplan, my children, Sam and Claudia, and my parents, Susan and Peter. Thank you.

About the Author

Co-founder and Executive Director at North Star: Self-Directed Learning for Teens in Sunderland, Massachusetts, Ken has been working intensively with teenagers and their families since 1991.

Previously a middle school social studies teacher, first in Prince George's County, Maryland, then in Amherst, Massachusetts, Ken left the Amherst school system to found North Star. He brought with him extensive education and training, including a Bachelor of Arts from Amherst College in Psychology, and an M.A.T. in Social Studies from Brown University.

Ken lives in Montague, Massachusetts, with his family. This is his first book.

Want To Learn More About Self-Directed Learning for Teens?

Author

You can contact Ken Danford via email at:
author@kennethdanford.com

Learn more about Ken at his author website:
KennethDanford.com

Watch Ken's TEDx Talk, "School is Optional," at
https://www.youtube.com/watch?v=Eq1rXdDWXrM&t=9s

You can see his Thrive 2020 Talk at
https://www.youtube.com/watch?v=pMb9KJxNi1k

Read Ken's article on Alumni Outcomes at
https://www.self-directed.org/tp/north-star-alumni/

North Star

Visit North Star's official website at: NorthStarTeens.org

Call the North Star office at: 413-582-0193

Visit North Star at:
45 Amherst Road, Sunderland, MA 01375

Liberated Learners
Visit Liberated Learners' official website at: LiberatedLearners.net

Email them at: info@liberatedlearners.net

Self-Directed Learning

Alternative Education Resource Organization:
http://www.educationrevolution.org

The Alliance for Self-Directed Education:
https://www.self-directed.org

Index